WHEN THE WELL RUNS DRY

Other books by Thomas H. Green, S.J.:

Opening to God: A Guide to Prayer

*Drinking From a Dry Well: A Sequel
to* When the Well Runs Dry

*Weeds Among the Wheat: Discernment:
Where Prayer and Action Meet*

*The Friend of the Bridegroom:
Spiritual Direction and the Encounter with Christ*

WHEN THE WELL RUNS DRY
Prayer Beyond the Beginnings

Thomas H. Green, S.J.

ave maria press AmP notre dame, indiana

Imprimi Potest:
Joaquin G. Bernas, S.J.
Provincial of the Province of the Philippines
October 15, 1978
Nihil Obstat:
Rt. Rev. Msgr. Benjamin L. Marino, P.A.
Vicar General - Chancellor
Imprimatur:
Jaime Cardinal L. Sin, D.D.
Archbishop of Manila
September 13, 1978

Founded in 1865, Ave Maria Press is a ministry of the Indiana Province of Holy Cross.

www.avemariapress.com

ISBN-10 1-59471-137-2   ISBN-13 978-1-59471-137-4

Cover and text design by David R. Scholtes

Printed and bound in the United States of America.

CONTENTS

PART ONE:

FROM KNOWING TO LOVING

PART TWO:

FROM LOVING TO TRULY LOVING

FOREWORD

. . .

It is no wonder to me that there are 170,000 copies of the first edition of this book in print. In it Thomas Green undertook to answer the need of many of the readers of his first book on prayer, *Opening to God*, which was written as an introduction to prayer. Many of Green's readers felt that he really touched their present experience of prayer only in the epilogue. These readers and many of his directees were not beginners in prayer. They had experienced the honeymoon period of beginning to engage in serious prayer, but they were experiencing difficulties. They needed some help, not only to understand the dark periods which now seemed their lot in prayer, but also to stay with prayer itself. *When the Well Runs Dry* was the answer to that cry for help. Its success is an indication of how helpful it turned out to be. It is, therefore, a great gift to those who take prayer seriously that Father Green and Ave Maria Press have decided to publish a second, revised edition of this important work.

Green draws not only on personal experience of dryness in prayer, his own and that of many directees, but also on some of the great masters of prayer, such as Teresa of Avila, John of the Cross, the author of the *Cloud of Unknowing*, and others. He helps modern pray-ers to understand that their own experience is mirrored in the discussions of these masters of prayer. He uses images from these masters to help us understand what is happening to us. And he keeps the focus of the reader and pray-er on the heart of the matter, namely the desire of God for a close relationship with each of his children. God, however, does not want us to relate to a distortion or an illusion, but to himself. Hence anyone who takes this relationship seriously will have periods, some of them quite long, when God seems absent, precisely because God wants us to know and love God, not consolations, not ideas about God.

Green uses images taken from the masters to illuminate the stages of prayer. The well image of the title, for example, comes from Teresa of Avila and is used to great effect. But the image that had the most effect on me was Green's own, the image of floating as opposed to swimming. When we float, we allow the current to take us where it will; when we swim, we choose the direction. It is difficult and frightening just to float, but it is only when we can allow ourselves to float in the current that is God that we are truly free and trusting. Green helps the reader to face the fears of floating into the embrace of God. No wonder this book is in the hands of so many people who are serious about prayer.

But even if we take into account the undeniable fact that this book is very helpful to those who experience dryness and darkness in prayer, it is still a wonder that there are over 170,000 copies of it in print. After all, it is not a primer on prayer, nor is it popularly written. I believe that there is something else at work in our world that has made this book such a necessity for so many. Recently I read an article by Sandra Schneiders[1] in which she makes the insightful point that many modern religious women (and, by extension, many modern seekers of God) are experiencing the Dark Night of the Senses and of the Soul described by John of the Cross. The upheavals precipitated by Vatican II and the renewal efforts for more than twenty-five years have not only changed many of the customs, rites, and ways of acting of all Catholics, but have also, she speculates, brought into sometimes harrowing personal question the very existence of God. The image of God we worshipped and prayed to is no longer credible, and many people find themselves wondering whether they have lost their faith. That they have not given up on God is evidenced by the fact that they seek help to find God even in this time of God's seeming absence. Schneiders makes a good case that we are individually and collectively in a state akin to the Dark Night described by John of the Cross. I wonder whether the immense popularity of *When the Well Runs Dry* is attributable to the fact that it met a need that is felt by many educated seekers of God in our modern culture.

At any rate, I am very pleased to have been asked to write the foreword to this revised edition. I recommend it highly and hope that it will continue to be of help to seekers of God for many years to come.

William A. Barry, S.J.

Preface to
the Second Edition

• • •

When my publishers told me they were planning a second edition of *When the Well Runs Dry*, and I began to reread the text with a view of updating it, I was happily surprised to discover how much it still rings true to my experience almost twenty years later. The sensation was that of a man married twenty years, rummaging about in the attic and coming upon the letters he wrote to his wife long ago—and realizing that he still meant every word he wrote in the honeymoon days. For me, the joy is in rediscovering the way the experience described in the book centered my life at that time—and in realizing that it still does.

In reflecting on how much revision I should attempt, I recalled a saying from my early years: "If it ain't broke, don't fix it." Since Ave Maria's purpose is to introduce a new generation of pray-ers to a book that has been a bestseller for them, it seemed wise to provide that new generation with the same book that has helped many of their elders. Certain changes, though, seemed likely to make the book more helpful to the current generation of readers. Primarily, three principal changes suggested themselves to me:

1) to update the footnote references: for example, using the more recent and more accessible Rodriguez and Kavanaugh translation of John of the Cross's (and Teresa of Avila's) writings, instead of the translation of Allison Peers, on which I was weaned, and which I came to love;

2) to use inclusive language, which I was unaware of at the time of the original book;

3) to insert section subheadings in the various chapters, so that the reader could more easily follow the flow of my thinking.

These are the principal changes I have made. I should also acknowledge the changes at Ave Maria. Eugene Geissler, the great gentleman with whom I dealt twenty years ago, and who is acknowledged in the original preface, has since retired. But he has worthy successors in Frank Cunningham, an old friend and now the publisher, and Robert Hamma, the editorial director. I also wish to thank another old friend from my seminary years, Fr. Bill Barry, S.J., for his truly gracious and perceptive foreword to the new edition.

Finally, I must thank all my directee "victims" of the past twenty years, who number in the hundreds. The ultimate test of the book is whether it also rings true to their experience. In fact, one happy discovery for me is that the book has proved a very helpful diagnostic tool in my work of direction. I often ask my directees to read all, or certain parts of it to see if it speaks to their experience. When it does they, and I, can be confident that they are on the right track in their life of prayer.

I hope that will be your experience too, and that you will pray for the diagnostician.

San Jose Seminary
Quezon City, Philippines
October 1, 1997 (Centenary of the Little Flower)

Preface to
the Original Edition

• • •

All the friends whom I have directed, who have shared their journey to God with me in the sixteen years since I was ordained a priest, have played a part in the writing of this book. So, too, have Mr. Segundiano Honorio, the secretary of San Jose Seminary, who cheerfully tackled the laborious task of deciphering my handwriting and typing the manuscript: also, two of my Jesuit brothers: Father Thomas O'Shaughnessy, whose careful reading eliminated many stylistic oddities and repetitions, and Father Bill Abbott, who kept my scriptural references honest and accurate and who often suggested apt references which I had not thought of; many of the San Jose diocesan seminarians, especially Ed Mercado and Willie Fabros, who, in their sharing of themselves and in their reading of the manuscript, have contributed immeasurably to my own understanding and my ability to explain the mystery of the "dry well"; and my own sister, Pidge James, who is still (as she was in *Opening to God*) my best and most constructive critic, despite the ocean now separating us. Two groups of friends served as willing "guinea pigs" for my airing of the ideas which were taking shape in this book, and contributed much by way of clarification and confirmation: the students in my course in Apostolic Prayer at Loyola School of Theology during the first semester of 1978; and the Ursuline Sisters who made a one-month "house of prayer" with me in Canberra, Australia, over Christmas of 1978.

Sister John Miriam Jones, SC, the Assistant Provost of the University of Notre Dame, with whom I have shared so much of my own thinking and experience concerning prayer, again (as with *Opening to God*) found the time to check the page proofs for me. Now, as then, she and I worked with Mr. Eugene Geissler, the book editor of Ave Maria Press, a real gentleman of the "old school" and a true friend. Sister Adele Nayal, OND,[1] did the sketch of a typical Filipino ground well—the type of well I contemplated as I began to think these thoughts about the time "when the well runs dry."

As I said above, all my "directees" have played a part in this book. Perhaps in acknowledging one in particular, I can express my gratitude to all. About three years ago I met a sister under mysterious and not very promising conditions. She urged me to "take a chance" on her and, reluctantly, I agreed. It was one of the best decisions I ever made—or, better, which the Lord ever made for me. Grace worked a miracle in her, and much more rapidly than I could have expected. Only this past year did I realize why she "blossomed" so quickly. She is now dying of kidney disease and the Lord knew she did not have much time. As I wrote the book, chapter by chapter, I was keenly conscious of how anxious she was to see it finished before she died. The fact that it is finished, and that she has seen it and liked it, and can now say her "nunc dimittis" in peace, is one of the nicest gifts the Lord has ever given me—and a sure sign of his love for her. Her name is Sister Stella Rosal, S.Sp.S. In dedicating the Well to her, I dedicate it to all who share her search and her wondrous discovery.

All that remains is to say the obvious: my debt to my mother and my father, from whom I first learned the meaning of love, is evident in every chapter of the book.

San Jose Major Seminary
Manila, Philippines
March 19, 1979 (Feast of San Jose)

INTRODUCTION:

To Tame and Be Tamed

• • •

On a beautiful, late spring day in June of '76 in Rochester, New York, I sat down to write some pages on prayer for beginners. The immediate purpose, in response to many people whom I had directed or to whom I had lectured on prayer, was to put in writing what I had been saying to them. They felt it would be helpful to have a written reminder to which they could refer at leisure. At that time, after seven years in the Philippines, I was on sabbatical at my own home in Rochester. Outside my window, the pine trees I loved as a boy now loomed taller than the house. My father was three years dead, but the bird feeder he had placed in the yard was still there as a tangible reminder of all the love he had lavished on this small piece of earth. My mother, thank God, was still very much present, busy about the house which, when we first moved into it in my teens, seemed like a palace to me because it had four bathrooms! Occasionally she and I took time for a cup of coffee or a trip to the store, but much of the time I sat in my room and tried to coax my thoughts on prayer from brain to pen to paper, happy in the knowledge that, after so many years, my mother was somewhere nearby. She was not really a good critic of what I wrote, although she was the first to read it and I did clarify many of the things I was trying to say after discussing them with her. But she was too supportive to be truly critical.

Thus it was that I was not really sure whether my ideas and experience would be of help to a wider audience. I had in mind that my writing might eventuate in a published book. But my primary audience was the seminarians and sisters and lay people I had been directing and teaching about prayer. My efforts were really a response to their requests. Moreover, it had a rather narrow and well defined focus. It was to be limited to the beginnings of the life of prayer, to be a guide for those seeking to lay the foundations for a solid interior life. It seemed to me there were many excellent works, classic and contemporary—such as those by John of the Cross and Teresa of Avila and Leonard Boase and Anthony Bloom and Thomas Merton—to guide those who were already serious and maturing in prayer. But I felt these works were usually too heavy for beginners, and often brought them more confusion and discouragement than enlightenment.

Apparently others felt as I did, for those three months of writing did result in a published book, *Opening to God*.[1] Many people told me that it did meet a real need for them, and I have been especially happy that it has been used fruitfully in many religious novitiates and with many lay prayer groups—precisely the beginners in prayer whom I had been hoping to be able to help.

Opening to God, however, also elicited one fairly common complaint. Those who had been praying for some years said: "You stopped just at the point where you were beginning to touch my experience. In the epilogue I found myself—and then you were finished!" I was not surprised at this, of course. The book was intended for beginners, and these friends of the Lord were beyond the beginnings of prayer. But when I suggested that they needed to go on to John of the Cross or Teresa of Avila or the *Cloud of Unknowing*, the invariable answer was, "But I'm not a mystic! Those authors are good for contemplatives, but I'm just an ordinary person." Often enough they had, in fact, looked into Teresa or John at one time (usually much too early in their prayer lives) and had been frightened away by John's austerity or confused by Teresa's wordiness. And so the treasures of the masters remained inaccessible to them now in their need.

• • •

Seeking God Beyond the Beginnings

Thus it was that I found myself, as a director, spending more and more time guiding people to these treasures, sharing as best I could the great enlightenment and support which I myself had found in certain key passages such as chapter 11 and following of Teresa's *Autobiography* and chapters 8–10 of Book I of John's *Dark Night of the Soul*. The Lord seemed to promote this venture by sending me even more people who needed just this kind of guidance, and by confirming its correctness by the fruits in their lives. Moreover, it seemed that it was not (as I had thought) enough simply to hand them a copy of John or Teresa. I should have realized this earlier, for I myself had puzzled over the masters for years, with a strong sense that the Lord was drawing me to them, and yet often with great frustration because of what I could not understand or accept. And rarely had I found "someone to guide me" (Acts 8:31). Like the Ethiopian whom Philip baptized, I did not see how I could "understand what I was reading" unless I found that "someone."

Although I have been blessed with at least three great Jesuit spiritual directors in my life thus far—Father Norris Clarke and Father Tom Clarke during my seminary years and Father Jim McCann in more recent years before his death—I never really did find the guidance I needed in prayer beyond the beginnings. It was not at all the fault of these good men; rather, it was the mark of the times in which I and they were formed. Praying generally meant meditation—something we do, our activity of analyzing the gospel and making applications to our own life situation and resolutions as to how we would serve Christ better. It was all very good as far as it went, but it did not go far enough. Specifically, it did not allow for the possibility that prayer might become less and less what we do and more and more what God does in us.

That this was what was happening in me during those early years I could scarcely recognize at the time. Even if I had been able to recognize the signs for what they were, I doubt I would have been able to believe that they were genuine. It seemed much more likely that my difficulty in doing anything at prayer—a difficulty which gradually became an impossibility—was due to my own sinfulness, to the many failings of which I became more and more acutely aware. When, in later years, I remembered the misery of those times, it made me all the more anxious to be of help to the many confused searchers whom the Lord sent my way. They came, of course, even before *Opening to God* was written. But only in the past two years did I begin to realize that it was not enough to put John or Teresa, or even a relatively recent writer like Boase, into their hands. Nor did it seem sufficient merely to guide them into John and Teresa in personal, face-to-face direction. By now many of my directees were scattered around the world, from Bolivia to Burundi to Brisbane. And even when we could meet personally, direction at this level of prayer proved exceedingly tricky and elusive. The passivity into which the Lord eventually leads us in prayer is so contrary to our natures, and the world into which we enter is so "upside down," that it seems the same lesson needs to be learned a thousand times over before it becomes truly our own.

So it was that this book, *When the Well Runs Dry*, came to be written. It is intended for those "beyond the beginnings," especially those whom I have had the privilege to direct, to help them to remember the lessons we have learned together. Above all they need to learn—to remember—that meditation/contemplation[2] is not normally a lifetime way of praying, even for active apostles. And they also need to remember that beyond meditation/contemplation is not a splendid oasis of Omar Khayyam filled with delights for the soul (which seems to be what most people understand by "mystic" or "contemplative"), but rather a vast desert of purifying dryness with, perhaps, occasional small oases to sustain the spirit. As we shall see, it is only when we come to love the desert, and to prefer it to the oases, that we are well on the way to God. It is an "upside-down" world indeed! We can well be forgiven for forgetting, for refusing to believe we are on the right road, when our throats are parched and our eyes are filled with sand!

This, then, is what *When the Well Runs Dry* is all about. The easiest part of the writing of the book was choosing the title. It is suggested by a beautiful image of St. Teresa of Avila and is explained in chapter 1 of this book. Whereas *Opening to God* was completed and in the hands of the publishers before the right title came to mind, I had the title of the new book long before I had the book! It not only catches perfectly what the book had to be about, but it also acknowledges the enormous personal debt which I owe to Teresa. In fact, when I began I intended the book to be merely an explanation of, and contemporary introduction to, some of the passages in Teresa and John and others which have been crucial to my own life and growth as a pray-er and as a director.

The Ultimate Test of Personal Experience

That is what I intended when I began writing. I would still hope that one major fruit of the book would be to lead others to find in the great authors on prayer the treasures which I myself have found there. Contrary to my expectations (and hopes), however, what came from my pen is not primarily an exegesis of these classic passages. Instead, the result is what I could only characterize as an attempt to describe my own experience, as pray-er and as director, of the way the Lord works in those he leads to the desert to speak to their hearts (see Hosea 2:16). Teresa and John, Boase and the author of the *Cloud of Unknowing* are my valued interpreters and guides, but the journey is my own (and that of my many "friends in the Lord"). I would have preferred to speak more objectively about the mystery of prayer, but it appears, from my experience at least, that prayer is truly a mystery (in Gabriel Marcel's sense: something we cannot objectify and view from a distance because it is intensely personal and involves our whole selves), and thus can only be described in a very personal and subjective way.

One advantage, though, of the more personal approach which evolved is that it has enabled me to see much more clearly what is distinctive and especially valuable in the great writers cited. Their experience of God has a universal quality which enables them to speak meaningfully to the friends of God in every age and culture: universal because it is the same Lord at work in all of us. But this universal experience is realized and expressed by each of them in a highly personal, truly unique way. Moreover, each of us responds to each of them in a uniquely personal way. Thus, Teresa is, and always will be, my "mother" in the life of prayer: her gentleness, her simplicity, her genius for capturing the deepest truth in the simplest, most comprehensible image—all these qualities drew me to her "at the breast," and seem even more wonderful as the years pass. She is, indeed, too wordy and rambling, as she herself frequently admits, but this can be an endearing fault in one who loves the Lord as ardently, and speaks with him and of him as unself-consciously as she does.

John of the Cross, by contrast, is intense and single-minded, a very great poet and also a first-rate theologian in the scholastic style of his day. His passion for God is every bit as intense as Teresa's, and much more lyrically expressed. He does not have her light touch, her self-deprecating wit. But when the time comes when we want the plain, unvarnished truth about where we stand with the Lord and ourselves (and it usually takes considerable maturity to desire or even to be willing to accept such bluntness), John is the man for us. He is, moreover, a master director of souls—the most perceptive and discerning I have ever encountered. The great passages in his writings (at least in my judgment) are those where he is describing and interpreting the way God normally works in the life of prayer. His theological explanations and scriptural exegesis often do not say much to me today; but a passage like chapters 8 to 10 of Book I of the *Dark Night of the Soul*, which I feel may well be the most important single thing ever written on prayer,[3] is as valuable today as when John wrote it. John, like the Lord he is describing, is an acquired taste. He is strong meat for the timid, and easily misunderstood by the neophyte, but once one has acquired maturity and a taste for him, most other food seems insipid by comparison.

There are, nonetheless, contemporary authors who can stand in John's company. Thomas Merton is one and Anthony Bloom another. The one whom I myself have found most helpful is Leonard Boase, S.J. His *Prayer of Faith* is really John of the Cross's "Dark Night of the Senses" in contemporary dress, and this contemporaneity is a special value of the book.[4] But Boase also brings a different and valuable perspective to the mystery of prayer beyond the beginnings. Unlike John and Teresa he is writing primarily and explicitly for those called to live an active, apostolic life in the world. His book makes abundantly clear that what John and Teresa describe is not only for "contemplatives," for cloistered monks and nuns who withdraw from the world. His insights on "praying always," and on the apostolic goal of the "prayer of faith" (Boase's name for the "dark night")—among many others—go straight to the heart of a Christian in the world today. Like Teresa and John, Boase has obviously lived what he describes.

Whereas these three authors have long been my companions on the journey of prayer, I discovered the *Cloud of Unknowing* in fairly recent years. It is a brief work, disarming and sometimes alarming in its brevity. Its great value for me was the revelation that the unknown author of the Cloud, a fourteenth-century Englishman who was probably a monk and was certainly a master spiritual director, was really describing the same experience of the same Lord as John and Teresa—and yet this experience was reflected through the prism of a very different personality, shaped in an English culture quite unlike the Spanish milieu of John and Teresa. The author of the Cloud is dry, ironic, understated, pragmatic—and a delight to read. In a way, he is the P. G. Wodehouse of spirituality![5]

• • •

The Challenge for the Reader— and for the Author

John remains my favorite and most trusted guide on the journey to the high places, but Boase provides the contemporary dress and the apostolic orientation. The Cloud (along with Teresa) provides the light touch and the common sense, the salt necessary to make palatable the strong meat of John. The mix is, as I said earlier, highly personal. Yet, it may be helpful to the reader to have this brief account of how I have responded to the great writers on prayer who have helped the Lord to shape my own vision of him and of what he is doing in prayer. No one else, probably, will see the masters in precisely the same way. Nor, in fact, would it be desirable that they do so. But my sharing may help you to discover your own vision, and to see the value of your unique and very personal synthesis of the best that the great teachers can share with you. This, after all, is the primary role of any good teacher (and of any good spiritual director, as John of the Cross stresses so strongly[6]). The synthesis of the student will always differ from that of his or her teachers, because it includes, in addition to all that the teachers can share, the unique element of personal experience.

If this book leads you, the reader, to your own integration of your own experience of prayer beyond the beginnings, it will have achieved its purpose. There are, of course, many other great masters of prayer who do not appear in these pages. This would be a serious flaw if the book were intended as a survey of spirituality or spiritualities, but our goal is a personal vision of the way God works in those he draws to love. What emerges from the authors cited is that his way is essentially the same—because it is always the same Lord of love working—in all the diverse temperaments and cultures on the face of the earth. Once we realize this, the primary need is not for more extensive reading about prayer, but for more intensive living of the life of prayer. In fact, at the risk of hurting the sales of my own book, I must say that the time eventually comes to stop reading and to start living. Too many gurus, no matter how good they be, will only dissipate our energies and retard our growth. John of the Cross says:

In matters pertaining to the soul, it is best for you, so as to be on the safe side, to have attachment to nothing and desire for nothing, and to have true and complete attachment and desire for him who is your proper guide, for to do otherwise would be not to desire a guide. And when one guide suffices, and you have one who suits you, all others are either superfluous or harmful.[7]

When John wrote this, he had in mind the spiritual director; books were still a relative rarity and few possessed the art of reading.

In our day, when we are bombarded by books and articles on every aspect of spirituality, his advice applies equally well to the guidance we seek in spiritual reading. Too much and too scattered reading, like too many directors, will be "either superfluous or harmful" for spiritual growth. The abundance of spiritual resources available to us today is indeed a blessing, provided only that we can select wisely those which help us to know the Lord. It is good to sample the riches in the early years of our prayer life; but once we discover what nourishes us, we must learn to sacrifice breadth for depth. Otherwise we will merely suffer from spiritual indigestion, and perhaps die of malnutrition!

It is a striking fact that we often learn more from teaching than we do from studying. The teacher, in attempting to communicate his knowledge and ideas to others, is himself or herself brought to a much greater clarity and depth of understanding about the matter in question. This, happily, has been my experience in all of the writing I have done. My own understanding of the way the Lord normally works in prayer has been greatly clarified and deepened as I attempted to explain it to others. As a result, I would now see three essential stages of growth in any solid interior life. These stages may vary in duration and intensity. They are, moreover, quite broad and allow for considerable variety in concrete experience. This is as it should be, since we are all unique personalities and the Lord of love encounters each of us in our uniqueness. But it is also true, as we have noted, that it is the same Lord we all encounter in prayer. The basic pattern common to our experience is, as we have said, due to this fact, that we all do encounter the same Lord, who is constant and faithful and true to his own nature. It is because of his consistency that we can even speak of common patterns of growth; and this in turn is what makes spiritual direction and the writings of the great spiritual masters meaningful for our own unique encounter with the Lord.

$$\bullet\ \bullet\ \bullet$$

Getting to Know the Other and Oneself

What, then, are these three basic stages of interior growth as I have discovered them? They correspond to the stages of growth in any human love relationship, and are best understood, I believe, by analogy to human love. The first stage is getting to know the Lord. We cannot really love what we do not know; there is no such thing as genuine love at first sight. When a "boy sees a girl across a crowded room," and finds himself instantly attracted to her, the most foolish thing he could do would be "to rush to her side and make her his own." If he did so, he would almost certainly wake up to find himself married to a stranger. The chances of a happy marriage resulting from such an impulsive decision would be very small indeed. There is such a thing as attraction, infatuation at first sight, but for that initial attraction to blossom into genuine love there must be a lengthy process of getting to know each other. "Rush to her side" . . . and ask her her name. Yes!

Timidity in responding to that initial impulse may well result in eternal loss. But to confuse the initial attraction with genuine love would almost certainly lead to a life of regret. It is the same with the Lord. With him, too, true love is grounded on a real knowledge, gradually acquired, of him and of ourselves. Being God, he could, it is true, circumvent this natural law of human love. But in my experience there is no evidence that he ever does so. Even Saul of Tarsus, so dramatically converted, had to spend a long time in the desert of Arabia discovering who this lover was who had captured him on the road to Damascus.

This first stage of getting to know the Lord (and ourselves) is the topic of *Opening to God*, and involves the practice of something like the meditation and/or contemplation described there, along with the related techniques for coming to quiet and for purifying the soul of all that blocks love. This stage may last for several years once we begin a serious life of prayer, or it may be considerably briefer if our home and school environment in our early years has already laid a solid foundation of knowledge of the Lord. In any event, it will eventually come to an end. We are not meant to spend our entire lives merely getting to know the Lord, any more than human lovers would spend their whole lives just seeking to know each other better.[8]

• • •

From Knowing to Loving

Thus, sooner or later, the one who prays faithfully moves into a second stage of prayer. I have characterized this as the move from knowing to loving, and it is the topic of the first part of the present book. Like human lovers, the center of the relationship between the one who prays and the Lord gradually moves from the head to the heart. Praying becomes much more affective and much less reflective. This stage of growth, whose emergence we hinted at in chapter 6 and the epilogue of *Opening to God*, is explained in chapter 1 below by means of St. Teresa of Avila's famous metaphor of the garden, where the flowers are the virtues and the water by which they live is prayer or, more properly, devotion (what St. Ignatius calls "consolation") in prayer.

The feelings, with all their mystery and ambiguity, become central to prayer. This presents the pray-er with a whole host of problems, not only because our feelings are ambivalent but because the object of our love is, in the case of prayer, One whom we cannot see or hear or touch in the ordinary way. He is the transcendent, the all-holy One, totally beyond our sensible grasp. At the beginning, perhaps, this will not be much of a problem for some, particularly those with good imaginations. Since we can image God in many ways—both in external media such as wood and stone and song, and also interiorly in our own imaginations. But the time will surely come when the well of our imagination runs dry and we must either be convinced that God is not the image we have of him or else we will take the loss of the image for the loss of God himself—and we will be tempted to abandon prayer as a hopeless endeavor.

Thus the second and third chapters of Part One treat two very important, but not immediately evident, implications of St. Teresa's image of the soul as the Lord's garden and affective prayer as the water by which the flowers in this garden are nourished and brought to maturity. Teresa was an eminently practical woman: She insisted often that beautiful feelings in prayer—the "experience of God" which so many seek today—are merely the water, merely a means. The end for which the water is intended is the virtues, the flowers in the garden. The mark of a good prayer life is not abundant consolation, but growth in the virtues. This point, which is particularly important in the life of the apostle and of the Christian in the world today, is the topic of chapter 2. What I try to spell out concretely and in some detail there is really an "unpacking" of the great test of authentic prayer which we find in the first epistle of John:

> Whoever says, "I know him" without keeping his commandments, is a liar. . . . Whoever claims to be in light but hates his brother is still in darkness. . . . Anyone who says "I love God" and hates his brother, is a liar, since whoever does not love the brother whom he can see cannot love God whom he has not seen (1 Jn 2:4, 9 and 4:20).

Thus the water is for the flowers; this is the first important implication of Teresa's metaphor. The second has to do with the fact that, even when we are clear on the distinction between the water of consolation and the flowers of virtue, and even when we do all we can to channel this water to the proper flowers, it may happen that we find there is no water in our prayer, no devotion, no consolation. I said this "may" happen; but, if the premise of this book is true, it would be more proper to say it surely will happen. That is why the book has been entitled "When" (and not "If ") the Well Runs Dry. Although they call it by different names, using different metaphors—the dry well of Teresa, the dark night of John of the Cross, the prayer of faith of Boase, the cloud of unknowing—all the great masters of prayer whom we cite recognize that the time will come when our intellects, our imaginations, our feelings dry up and cease to be of help. It seems then that we have lost God; but the purpose of the whole experience is rather to reveal to us that God, the Lord we love, is not to be identified with any of these created means—that to learn to distinguish him from every human mode by which we grasp him is not to lose him (as will surely appear to be the case at first), but truly to find him.

This God who is not in the wind, nor in the earthquake nor in the fire was finally experienced by Elijah in a tiny

31

whispering sound (1 Kgs 19:9–12). He is the Lord of the encounter and it is he who determines when and how we shall experience him. I have used Teresa's image of the first periodic drying of the well of consolation to explain the way the Lord asserts his sovereignty in our prayer. This is the topic of chapter 3, which bears the same title as the whole book: "When the Well Runs Dry." The dryness is sporadic; there are times when God is close and we are consoled, and times when he seems far away. The important point is that we don't seem to be able to do anything to control the water of devotion—he is teaching us to let him be "the Boss."[9]

• • •

Midlife, When Drought Becomes Normal

Chapter 3 is still part of the move "from knowing to loving," from the head to the heart. The periodic drying up of the well of devotion teaches us to let the Lord control the flow. But the good times, the fruitful times, still seem to us to be the times when the water of consolation is flowing freely. We value and desire them more as they become less frequent and less subject to our manipulation. But what if the drought became the normal state of things? What if the well really ran dry, not just occasionally but permanently? This would mean that God would seem to have withdrawn from us forever, and this just when we have become deeply attached to him! Before we knew about the well, we had no concern for the water it provided. Now that we have learned to thirst for that water, it seems especially cruel that it should be turned off at the source. Why would the Lord treat in such a way those who have come to love and desire him? To those who have never experienced it, it is indeed inconceivable that he would do so. But he does! Teresa told him it was not at all surprising he has so few friends, considering how he treats the few friends he does have. Many of his other friends, whom I have been privileged to direct, have echoed her complaint. Why does the Lord deal with them so "cruelly"?

Part Two of this book is my attempt to answer that question, and to encourage those friends of the Lord whom he loves enough to share with them his own thirst on Calvary. This part is entitled "From Loving to Truly Loving." The title implies that the affective love of which we spoke in Part One may not really be love at all—or to put it more accurately, may be but a pale shadow of the genuine love which we discover in the drought, in the dark night. It was good to move from the head to the heart, but now we must learn by experience that "heart" is an ambivalent word: it involves our emotions, but it also involves our will.

The emotions, those feelings which have a strong element of sense and imagination in them, are a good and necessary part of the whole human being. But they are essentially self-centered. They grasp at whatever pleases and gratifies them. They are not immoral, but they are amoral. That is, they do not make moral judgments about the rightness or wrongness of what is presented for their gratification—they simply go for whatever attracts them and promises them pleasure. Thus, love which is strongly emotional is essentially self-seeking, concerned with its own pleasure and delight. It is this kind of "love" which makes for intense courtships and short marriages, since even in marriage the well of emotion will surely run dry as the honeymoon is followed by the ordinary, routine days which make up most of our lives. Second honeymoons are a splendid idea, a very valuable way to revitalize and deepen a marriage—but only if they enable us to return home with a deeper appreciation of the ordinary days to come.

The central point of chapters 4 and 5 is that much the same is true in our relationship to God. One sure mark of genuine spiritual growth, I think, is a growing preference for the ordinary days of our life with God. We gradually begin to realize that it is when nothing seems to be happening that the most important things are really taking place. The clay is molded into a thing of beauty quietly and imperceptibly (chapter 4); and our "work" at this time—we who now become the clay in the hands of the divine Potter—is really to learn to "do nothing gracefully" (chapter 5), perhaps the hardest and most demanding thing we ever learn to do.

• • •

Floating in the Sea of God

If authors are permitted to have favorite passages in their own writings, my choice would be chapter 6 of the Well.[10] I suppose it is because here I felt I had to let go of the hands of John and Teresa and Boase—and strike out on my own. It seemed to me, as a director, that two questions remained unanswered once I had shared with mature pray-ers the best that I could cull from the masters: Where is this experience of darkness, of the dry well, really leading? What is its relevance for the committed apostle of Christ at the dawn of the twenty–first century, in an era which has seen and affirmed (as in Vatican II and in the synods which have followed) the necessary link between witnessing to faith and promoting social justice?

The first question—the goal of it all—is what I seek to answer in chapter 6. Perhaps it is my favorite because I feel that at long last I have answered it, at least to my own satisfaction! The answer emerged in terms of a metaphor: floating. Chapter 6 is essentially an extended development of that metaphor. It seeks to show that the Lord's work is all directed to teaching us to float in the sea which is himself, and that it is really, though paradoxically, the floaters and not the swimmers who get places and accomplish great things for the sake of the kingdom of God. It is here, too, that the answer to the second question becomes evident: It is only in floating that one really witnesses to faith and promotes justice in a Spirit-filled way. I myself am very far from being a good floater in the Sea of God. But I think now I can see the way I must go. I think I now understand why it is the Gandhis and the Hammarskjolds, the Mother Teresas and the Martin Luther Kings (and Popes John XXIII, Paul VI, and John Paul II, thanks be to God!) who have really touched the conscience of the twentieth century. The epilogue of this book is my own attempt to put into words what I believe they discovered—the real meaning of "Blessed are the poor in spirit."

I hope that what I have found will resonate in the hearts of at least some of you who read it. A book like this has to be read with the heart and not with the eyes, for, as the wise fox told the little prince: "It is only with the heart that one can see rightly; what is essential is invisible to the eye." If you find something of that "essential invisible" here, I will indeed be very happy. And I promise to remember and take to heart those other words of the wise old fox: "You become responsible, forever, for what you have tamed. You are responsible for your rose. . . ."[11] It is a responsibility I would happily share with the Lord (who is, of course, the ultimate fox), especially since it is so clear that, inevitably and necessarily, the rose also becomes forever responsible for the little prince!

PART ONE
FROM KNOWING
TO LOVING

1

WELLS AND STREAMS AND
CLOUDBURSTS

• • •

My life has been lived in places where the supply of water is abundant and the water itself is good. But there are times here in Manila—especially when new, larger pipelines are being laid to meet the ever expanding needs of the city—when there is no water for a day or two. It is a frustrating experience, particularly for Filipinos who, if anything, are more addicted to cleanliness than Americans. Usually, when things are normal, we take the water for granted. But when the pipes run dry our consciousness is raised. I, for one, feel thirsty and sticky and sweaty as soon as I discover there is no water! And all of us here say we would much rather go without electricity than without water.

Jesus lived in a world where water was a much more precious commodity. Not only was it scarce, but much of what was available was dangerous—stagnant water was the breeding ground for some of the most feared diseases. For Jesus and for his people, the value of water—good water, flowing water, what he called "living" water, was very great. It is not surprising, then, that he so frequently uses water as a symbol of life and salvation, a symbol already prominent in Isaiah, Jeremiah, and the Psalms.[1] Yahweh is the source of living waters and he leads his chosen ones to drink from the waters of life and to lie down in peace by "restful waters."

The same beautiful symbol, with its roots in the daily life of a people surrounded by the desert, dominates John's vision of eternal life at the end of the Book of Revelation: "Then he said to me, 'It has already happened. I am the Alpha and the Omega, the Beginning and the End. I will give water from the well of life free to anybody who is thirsty'" (Rev 21:6). This is the promise of the God of love, and in his final vision John sees its eternal fulfillment: "The angel showed me the river of life, rising from the throne of God and of the Lamb and flowing crystal clear. Down the middle of the city streets, on either bank of the river, were the trees of life, which bear twelve crops of fruit in a year, once each month, and the leaves of which are a cure for the nations" (Rev 22:1–2).

The book of Revelation is a mysterious work. It is persecution literature, written to encourage a church threatened by enemies—and hence it is in "code."[2] But the meaning of the "river of life" is clear enough when we recall the Old Testament significance of "living water" and when we also realize the part played by water in Jesus' teaching in St. John's Gospel.

Jesus tells Nicodemus that "no one can enter into God's kingdom without being begotten of water and Spirit" (Jn 3:5). His encounter with the woman of Samaria is a beautiful "comedy of errors"—an example of the "irony" so typical of St. John—with the woman talking about the "living" water which flows from the earth and Jesus talking about the living water within a person: "No one who drinks the water that I shall give will ever be thirsty again: the water that I shall give will become a spring of water within, welling up for eternal life." The woman still misunderstands; the discussion of water concludes with her saying: "Sir, give me some of that water so I may never be thirsty or come here again (to the well) to draw water" (Jn 4:14–16).

The woman's confusion is understandable; it is a new and strange thing the Lord is saying to her. But as John and the early church meditated on the water become wine at Cana (Jn 2), the water that healed the blind man (Jn 9), the beautiful incident of the washing of the disciples' feet at the Last Supper (Jn 13), then the symbolism of water became more and more central to the teaching of Jesus. It was not at all surprising that water should flow from the side of Jesus—"One of the soldiers pierced his side with a lance and immediately there came out blood and water" (Jn 19:34) as the concluding incident of the drama of Calvary. Jesus dies that we may have life; the eternal life within him flows out upon the church and upon each one who believes in Jesus, becoming "a spring of water within, welling up for eternal life."

The water symbolism of Jesus has continued to live in the church, particularly in the baptismal liturgy. Like any great symbol it is drawn from our ordinary experience; but it "works" for us as a symbol (i.e., a visible sign pointing to an invisible, interior reality) because it "echoes" the supreme symbol of the incarnation, in which the invisible reality of God was made visible to us in Jesus, a flesh-and-blood human being like ourselves. Jesus is the symbol, the sacrament par excellence, because he makes visible to us the Father who dwells in unapproachable light. Philip expresses the desire, and the frustration, of every Christian who seeks to reach out to a God he cannot see when he says, "Lord, show us the Father and then we shall be satisfied." And Jesus replies: "Have I been with you all this time, Philip, and you still do not know me? Anyone who has seen me has seen the Father" (Jn 14:8–9). For Paul, this means that Jesus "is the image of the invisible God" (Col 1:15), in whom are all the treasures of the wisdom and knowledge of the Father. Once Jesus has come and dwelt among us, it becomes doubly true that, as Paul proclaimed, "the invisible existence of God and his everlasting power have been clearly seen by the mind's understanding of created things" (Rom 1:20). This, above all, sets Christianity apart from any religion in which the things of this world are illusory and spirituality is achieved in a flight from our concrete experience. The most ordinary things—like water—reveal God, if only we have the eyes to see.

• • •

Metaphors as Maps

Like all great symbols, water is very rich in its symbolic possibilities. We never exhaust all that it can reveal to us, and the friends of God continually find new meaning in it.[3] Thus it is not surprising that St. Teresa of Avila, when she sought to describe her own experience of the "stages" of interior growth, should turn to a water-metaphor to express her meaning. The water image she uses has become perhaps the most famous metaphor in the history of Christian spirituality. In my work as a director of souls I have found it even today the best way to explain to those who pray the mysterious ways of God in "prayer beyond the beginnings." Now it is the centerpiece of this book, in which I hope to share with other friends of God what I have learned about his mysterious ways.

Before we turn to Teresa's metaphor, however, it might be good to say a word about books on prayer and stages of growth. Many good souls are uninterested in such analyses of the way God works. As they have said to me, "I don't want to be introspective, to analyze what 'stage' I'm in. I'm happy just to pray, to keep my eyes on the Lord and not be looking over my shoulder at myself and figuring out what 'mansion' I am in. All that seems too self-centered and analytical." In my experience this is a valid objection. One of the great hazards of the interior life is that we go to find God and we end up talking to ourselves. There is a fine line between prayer and introspection, and I suspect that all of us who pray cross that line continually and, without even realizing it, get caught up in sterile self-analyses and conversations with ourselves about ourselves. This is surely not prayer, and yet any discussion of the stages of interior growth runs the hazard of encouraging precisely this kind of centering on self. How then can we justify such a discussion?

The answer, it seems to me, is best found in another metaphor suggested by one of the best contemporary books on prayer, Leonard Boase's *The Prayer of Faith*. Boase compares books on prayer to maps, and he says we use them in precisely the way we use a map.[4] It is a tool to help us get where we are going. To become preoccupied with analyzing our stage of prayer is like being hypnotized by the map, making it the center of our attention and forgetting about the journey and the goal. This is certainly not good.

Yet, maps have a real value. We consult them to reassure ourselves we are on the right road. If I want to drive from Los Angeles to San Francisco, studying the map won't get me one step closer to my goal. But if, as I journey, I find myself in Chicago, it might be a good idea to consult the map to see whether I am really on the right route. If I refuse to do so, out of a misguided aversion to the artificiality of maps, I may end up wandering aimlessly forever, without ever reaching my destination. We don't paste the map on the windshield and contemplate it as we travel; we would surely crash. But it is a very good idea to have the map beside us on the seat, for consultation when we are in doubt.[5]

Teresa's Garden

Teresa's metaphor of the ways of drawing water, then, is a map for those seeking to journey to God. It is composed by one who knows the route well: the landmarks, the confusing intersections, the less-traveled but surer shortcuts. It is not meant as a substitute for the journey but as a guide for those who have actually left their comfortable armchairs and set out on the road, drawn by someone they only vaguely know, to a destination they can scarcely imagine.[6] On such a mysterious journey, a good guide is not only helpful but virtually essential. Let us see, then, the map of the journey which Teresa draws from her own experience.

She is seeking to explain to the beginner what it will mean—"what we have to do, the labor this will cost us, whether the labor is greater than the gain, and for how long it must last"[7]—to commit oneself seriously to a life of prayer. She says:

> The beginner must realize that in order to give delight to the Lord he is starting to cultivate a garden on very barren soil, full of abominable weeds. His Majesty pulls up the weeds and plants good seed. Now let us keep in mind that all of this is already done by the time a soul is determined to practice prayer and has begun to make use of it. And with the help of God we must strive like good gardeners to get these plants to grow and take pains to water them so that they don't wither but come to bud and flower and give forth a most pleasant fragrance to provide refreshment to this Lord of ours. Then he will often come to take delight in this garden and find his joy among these virtues.

This is the image Teresa will use for the next eleven chapters of her *Autobiography* to describe the life of prayer. It is a simple image: The soul that begins to pray is like an assistant gardener (a "tenant farmer" we would say in the Philippines) whose task it is to tend a garden owned and planted by the Lord God. The primary job of the tenant and the heart of Teresa's metaphor—is to water the garden, so that the plants may live and thrive. As we will see shortly, it is the four ways of drawing water for the garden which provide the framework of Teresa's discussion of the stages of the life of prayer. But first, let us note some very important points which are almost concealed from us by the very simplicity of the picture Teresa evokes.

Most basic, and ultimately most important to the beginner, is the fact that it is the Lord, and not the one who prays, who chooses the plot of land for the garden. Jesus insists on the same point: "You did not choose me, no, I chose you; and I commissioned you to go out and bear fruit" (Jn 15:16). In the discourse on the bread of life, where Jesus confronts the disciples for the first time with the challenge of decisive commitment, he affirms three times that it is only by the "drawing" of the Father that any person comes to faith: "No one can come to me unless drawn by the Father who sent me; and I will raise that person up on the last day" (Jn 6:44; see also 6:37, 65). These words of Jesus are very familiar to many Christians, and yet how difficult it is to believe them in the concrete circumstances of our lives! We are prone to think that it is we who choose to come to God, that it is we who decide to pray seriously, to make a good retreat, to follow a religious vocation—even to be a practicing Christian. In a sense, of course, this is true. That is, God never forces us to come to him; he always invites us and waits for our free response. But the point is that he always takes the initiative: it is impossible to pray or to be a believing Christian unless the Lord is first drawing me, inviting me, unless he gives me the grace to respond freely to his invitation. "His Majesty pulls up the weeds and plants good seed." Even the desire for God, as we shall have occasion later to stress, is a clear sign of God's presence. We cannot even desire to encounter him unless he is at work in us drawing us.

Another crucial point in Teresa's metaphor is that the water is for the plants. The water is prayer—more precisely, our experience of God in prayer, often called "consolation"—and the good plants in the garden are the virtues. Teresa is a contemplative, given to a life primarily devoted to prayer. Yet, even for her, prayer is not an end in itself. It is for the virtues, just as the water in the garden is for the flowers. We do not draw water just for the sheer joy of drawing water but in order that we may water the garden and keep the plants alive and growing. Similarly we do not seek the experience of God in prayer merely for its own sake but in order that the virtues in our lives may live and grow.

What are these virtues? Faith, hope and love, humility, self-forgetfulness, sensitivity to the needs of others (the fraternal love of which John speaks constantly in his gospel and first epistle), zeal for the glory of God and for the extension of the kingdom of Christ—these are the principal virtues, to which St. Teresa frequently refers throughout her writings. If these are growing in us, our prayer life is quite genuine and fruitful, no matter how "dry" it may be. If we cannot see any real growth in these virtues, something is wrong no matter how abundant the water of consolation may be. We may well suspect that the well is poisoned if the flowers die despite a steady supply of the water of consolations.[8]

It is, in fact, our growth in the virtues which "attracts" the Lord to us after he has first planted them in us. Thus, while everything depends on the grace of God—both to begin to pray and to persevere in a life of prayer once begun—he always leaves room for our free response. Love is a dialogue, and we cannot have a dialogue unless both persons are speaking. Moreover, as St. Ignatius Loyola points out in the *Spiritual Exercises*, this is a dialogue of actions more than of words. Ignatius says that love is shown more in deeds than in words, and that genuine love involves a mutual exchange of gifts.[9] Even in loving God we are givers as well as receivers. Our gifts, the deeds which show love, are the virtues which we nurture in our lives. Thus, Teresa can say: "And with the help of God we must strive like good gardeners to get these plants to grow and take pains to water them so that they don't wither but come to bud and flower and give forth a most pleasant fragrance to provide refreshment to this Lord of ours. Then he will often come to take delight in this garden and find his joy among these virtues."

• • •

Four Ways of Watering God's Garden

The Lord is the gardener; we are the assistants or "tenants"; the plants are the virtues and the water is that experience of God in prayer which we call "consolation."[10] Our task is to water the garden which God has planted. This brings Teresa to the central point of her metaphor:

> But let us see now how it must be watered so that
> we may understand what we have to do, the labor
> this will cost us, whether the labor is greater than
> the gain, and for how long it must last. It seems
> to me the garden can be watered in four ways.
> You may draw water from a well (which is for
> us a lot of work). Or you may get it by means of
> a water wheel and aqueducts in such a way that
> it is obtained by turning the crank of the water
> wheel. (I have drawn it this way sometimes—the
> method involves less work than the other, and you
> get more water.) Or it may flow from a river or a

stream. (The garden is watered much better by this means because the ground is more fully soaked, and there is no need to water so frequently—and much less work for the gardener.) Or the water may be provided by a great deal of rain. (For the Lord waters the garden without any work on our part—and this way is incomparably better than all the others mentioned.) [11]

There are, then, four ways of getting water for the garden: by drawing it up from the well by hand; by the use of a "water wheel" (today we would say "a pump"), where the mechanical apparatus does much of the work for us, and we get much more water with much less work; by a stream flowing through the garden, so that the water is readily available and merely has to be channeled to the roots of the plants; and, finally, by a heavy rain, where the water gets to the plants without our doing anything. In the following eleven chapters, Teresa explains how each of these four ways applies to prayer. She has a double purpose in mind. She does intend to provide a sort of map for those who give themselves to the journey of prayer, but she is writing her autobiography principally so that her spiritual director can make a judgment concerning the authenticity of her own extraordinary experiences in prayer.[12] This latter, primarily autobiographical purpose does not much concern us here. What we are interested in is the description, the map, which Teresa gives of the ways God normally works in the prayer life of those who sincerely seek him. In my experience, it is a remarkably accurate description of the way the Lord usually works. What I should like to do, then, is to discuss these four ways of drawing water, indicating, with the help of Teresa's comments, how they apply to the spiritual journey of every individual who prays.

Laborious Beginnings: Drawing by Hand

The first way of getting water for the garden is by drawing it from the well by hand. This is hard work, and we get very little water for the labor involved. Once, when I was on retreat in Antique, I remember watching the gardener draw water from a well near the house. The well was about forty feet deep, and the bucket was small. As he lowered the bucket to the bottom, filled it, and then drew it up carefully to avoid spilling too much, I was struck by the aptness of Teresa's image. Each small bucket, never completely full after the shaky journey up from the well, was then carried across the yard to water a few plants. The water which it took several minutes to draw and carry could be poured out in a few seconds on the thirsty plants baking under a tropical sun. I remember thinking how boring the gardener's work must be—the endless repetition of the same laborious process. And for such meager results!

This is precisely the image Teresa intended to evoke. It corresponds to our beginnings in prayer, to what we called in chapter 6 of *Opening to God* "The Ways of Prayer of Beginners," meditation and contemplation. The laborious drawing and carrying corresponds to our labor, using our understanding and imagination, to get to know the Lord. The small amount of water is the occasional moment of "contact" with the Lord which such labor brings. As we saw in *Opening to God*, beginners have traditionally been taught to devote some moments at the end of prayer to colloquy, to talking with the Lord about those things we have been considering or contemplating. This is the time when all our labor in thinking and imagining bears some fruit in devotion, in a sense of contact with the Lord, in an experience of his being present. Often for the beginner the "water" obtained is very little for the labor expended. And we wonder if it is all worthwhile.

For Teresa, it is eminently worthwhile. The labor expended has a definite purpose, even though we do not yet see the results. She says: "Beginners in prayer, we can say, are those who draw water from the well. This involves a lot of work on their own part, as I have said. They must tire themselves in trying to recollect their senses. Since they are accustomed to being distracted, this recollection requires much effort."[13] The problem is that we lead scattered, shallow lives, concerned about many things but never going very deeply into any one thing. The first problem in really learning to pray is to get serious about it—about the Lord. Small children have a very short attention span. That is why it is such a challenge to teach the primary grades—you have to have a new project for them about every thirty seconds. As we mature, our attention span becomes longer, but we still tend, like Martha, to be "bothered about many things" and to find it hard to focus on the one thing necessary. The college student studying in front of the TV, with people constantly coming and going in the room, is an apt symbol for our distracted age. Even at the natural level people realize this is not good or healthy; that is why there is such an emphasis on techniques for self-reflection today. They are laborious, but they produce a quieting, a centering which makes the effort worthwhile for their practitioners.

Teresa sees the same kind of centering as necessary for genuine prayer. She goes on to say that beginners "need to get accustomed to caring nothing at all about seeing or hearing, to practicing the hours of prayer." In chapter 4 of *Opening to God* we discussed the ways of doing this under the rubric of "coming to quiet." It is, as we said there, the essential preliminary step in a genuine life of prayer. But Christian prayer is not just another technique for achieving quiet and concentration, even in the initial meditative stages of drawing water by hand from the well. Even here, more is happening and there are other reasons why prayer is laborious. Teresa indicates two:

> beginners need to get accustomed . . . to thinking on their past life. Although these beginners and the others as well must often reflect upon their past, the extent to which they must do so varies, as I shall say afterward. In the beginning such reflection is even painful, for they do not fully understand whether or not they are repentant of their sins. If they are, they are then determined to serve God earnestly. They must strive to consider the life of Christ — and the intellect grows weary in doing this.

Thus, in addition to the effort to come to quiet, there are two other reasons why the beginnings of prayer are laborious: all good prayer is based on honest self-knowledge, and it is painful for us to confront ourselves honestly; also, it takes real effort to get to know Christ, particularly since we do not encounter him (see him and touch him and hear him) as we encounter another human being. For both reasons, most people prefer a distracted, scattered life. They will say, "How I wish I had the time for quiet reflection and leisure!" but when the time comes, they really do not know what to do with themselves. Even with all my years of praying, I can see this in myself. The desire for quiet is very real, but when the time comes that I am free, how difficult it can be to really focus the leisure, to confront myself and the Lord honestly and deeply. Leisure can so easily degenerate into an idle, daydreaming replay of past and future activities. If this is true of me, how much more for the beginner who has not known the Lord, who still does not know whether there is any water in the well to justify the labor and the pain?

Yet, Teresa is right. There is no solid interior life except one which is grounded on a genuine, honest knowledge of myself and of Jesus Christ. We cannot love what we do not know. To love the Lord we must first come to know him in Jesus Christ. To love ourselves properly (which is also essential to any genuine spirituality) we must come to know ourselves as we truly are. This is the labor of the first way of drawing water. Normally it is the task with which we begin our tenancy of the garden which the Lord has entrusted to us.

We have already described the ways of prayer of beginners in *Opening to God*: meditation and contemplation. In meditation we use our understanding, our reasoning, to come to a deeper knowledge of the God we are drawn to love. In contemplation we seek the same knowledge, but by the use of our imagination—"reliving" imaginatively the events of the Lord's life, and seeing ourselves, with our own concrete personal history, as part of these events. Both are good ways to accomplish the threefold labor which Teresa says is necessary to the beginner. Which one we use—meditation or contemplation—depends much on our own temperament, the grace of the moment, the particular scripture passage we are considering. In both cases the primary source is the gospels since, for the Christian, Jesus is the revelation of God: "Have I been with you all this time, Philip, and you still do not know me? Whoever has seen me has seen the Father" (Jn 14:9). The problem is that we have not seen Jesus in the flesh as Philip did. We are those blessed ones of whom Jesus spoke to Thomas who have not seen and yet have believed. How do we know the Father through Jesus? As John has said in the first conclusion to his Gospel, it is precisely for us that the scriptures have been written, that we might "see" Jesus in the sacred word and in this way come to know the Father: (These signs) "are recorded so that you may believe that Jesus is the Christ, the Son of

God, and that believing this you may have life through his name" (Jn 20:31). The signs in the Gospels become real in our own lives via meditation and contemplation. They give light and meaning to the "signs" which Jesus works in each of our lives, too. They lead to faith, and faith leads to life in Jesus' name.

•••

The Pump: More Water, Less Labor

Thus meditation and contemplation are just the beginning of the Christian life of prayer. They should lead to a living faith, to a lived experience of God. In terms of Teresa's metaphor, all the labor at the well is not for its own sake, but in order that we may draw the water of the experience of God which we seek—that water which becomes a living fountain within us welling up to provide eternal life (Jn 4:14). This is why manuals of prayer have traditionally stressed the "colloquy," the time of talking to the Lord from the heart about what we have seen in our reflection . . . even for beginners. Even when the well is being dug we should not lose sight of the water which is the reason for our labor. We don't dig for the sake of digging, but in order to drink of the waters of life. As the digging proceeds, our labor may be rewarded by a mere trickle of water. But even this trickle is important. It is a harbinger, a promise of the abundant flow beneath the surface, and we are drawn on by our hope of that promised abundance.

The danger at this point is that we are impatient for quick results. Our enthusiasm is stirred by a good retreat, an inspiring sermon, or the example of a friend. But if there is no proper follow-up, it can quickly wane as we realize the demands of day-by-day fidelity to quiet, undramatic growth. Many people's lives are filled with projects enthusiastically begun but never finished. In the Philippines we have an attitude we call *ningas cogon* or "cogon fire." The cogon is the tough field grass, abundant here, which burns fiercely for a short time and then quickly dies out. The enthusiasm of many who begin to pray, unfortunately, is like the ningas cogon. God's work is not like the cogon fire, but rather like the fire in the forest which smolders imperceptibly for days or weeks in the roots of the trees.

If we persevere patiently, the time comes when our hope is realized, when the water of the experience of God begins to flow freely and with relatively little meditative labor. This is Teresa's second way of drawing water "by means of a water wheel and aqueducts in such a way that it is obtained by turning the crank of the water wheel." As she comments: "I have drawn it this way sometimes—the method involves less work than the other, and you get more water."[14] The modern equivalent of the water wheel would be a manual pump. It is much easier to draw water with a pump because the machinery does much of our work for us. A few strokes with the pump handle start the water flowing, and then the flow continues easily with just an occasional, one-handed stroke.

How does the image of the pump apply to prayer? When we begin to draw the water of prayer in this second way, we still go to the well of meditation and contemplation. We still use our own faculties, our reasoning and imagination, to seek the experience of God. But much less labor with our faculties produces much more water. I have seen this myself with beginners in prayer. In giving a retreat to those who are just beginning, I might suggest for their prayer chapter 6 of St. John, the discourse of Jesus on the bread of life. A few hours later they would be back to ask what to do next. "I finished chapter 6, and also did chapter 7 and 8. Where do I go from here?" "Did you find the matter fruitful?" "Oh, yes, I got many good ideas from it, but now I'm ready to move on." A year or two later, I might suggest the same chapter

6 to the same beginners. This time their experience would be quite different: They would return the next day to say: "Chapter 6 was so rich and fruitful I was not able to finish it. I spent the whole day on the first part. The scripture you suggest is too much for the time we have to pray."

What has happened in the intervening year? The water has begun to flow freely. Comparatively little effort on the part of our reasoning and imagination has produced much consolation. The Lord has provided a pump to multiply the results of our efforts. Perhaps for the first time we realize the meaning and the joy of prayer as an encounter with God in love.

I remember well my own days as a Jesuit novice in 1950. Those were the golden days of abundant vocations, and we were about 125 novices crowded into two large study halls. Each of us had a desk and, beside the desk, a wooden kneeler. In those days kneeling at prayer was de rigeur. (If one ventured not to kneel but to stand or sit, he was very likely to receive a summons from the novice master discreetly inquiring if he were sick!) How many mornings I knelt there, trying to meditate but obsessed by my aching knees, wondering what prayer was all about and whether I would ever really discover its meaning! My reflections were labored and the labor produced very little water of devotion. Worse still, as I looked around me the others seemed to have discovered some inner spring of ecstasy which was totally alien to me. Worst of all, one of the novices (now a fine priest and a good friend) always seemed to be writing down some profound insight or feeling in his journal. His apparent success made my own failure all the more wretched! I hated him and all the rest of them! What had they found that was forever out of my reach?

As I was to learn years later, most of them hadn't found anything. They were thinking the same thoughts I was and to them I looked like the one who had found the secret of it all! I have told this story many times over the years, and the type of laughter it evoked made clear that my hearers knew from their own experience what I was talking about. The happy part of the story is that they also knew the sequel: If we persevere in this strange venture, the day finally comes when we discover for ourselves what it is all about. Suddenly, perhaps, the water of consolation begins to flow. We are provided with an invisible pump to multiply our feeble energies, and we ourselves realize the secret which those around us had apparently found ahead of us. Everything comes alive; every line of scripture and every bit of creation speak to us of the God of love and the love of God. It is the springtime of our interior life, rich with the promise of discoveries to be made. Sometimes when this happens in a retreat, a seminarian will say to me: "The scripture passages you suggested for my prayer were just the right ones! They spoke to me and touched me deeply." However, I know that once the pump begins to work, any scripture passage or any event would reveal God. At that point, as I have sometimes said to them, I could give them the telephone directory to pray over, and they would find God in every name on every page!

• • •

Am I Really Praying?

This is the first real breakthrough in the interior life. We begin to realize what it means to say that prayer is loving and not thinking. Teresa calls it the prayer of quiet, and she has this to say about it:

> Let us speak now of the second manner, ordained by the Lord of the garden, for getting water; that is, by turning the crank of a water wheel and by aqueducts, the gardener obtains more water with

less labor; and he can rest without having to work constantly. Well, this method applied to what they call the prayer of quiet is what I now want to discuss.

Here the soul begins to be recollected and comes upon something supernatural because in no way can it acquire this prayer through any efforts it may make. True, at one time it seemingly got tired turning the crank, and working with the intellect, and filling the aqueducts. But here the water is higher, and so the labor is much less than that required in pulling it up from the well. I mean that the water is closer because the grace is more clearly manifest to the soul.[15]

This makes clear why Teresa would refer to this new way of praying as the prayer of quiet. The one who prays "obtains more water with less labor; and he can rest without having to work constantly." There is a newfound joy simply in being still in the presence of the Lord, just as good friends find joy simply in being together. They are not self-conscious or nervous about silences. They don't plan their conversation or analyze their relationship. They don't really "think about" each other much when they are together. They just are, and they are happy to be together, whatever may be happening. Talking and silence are spontaneous and easy and relaxed—not labored or artificial. I have often used the following example: Suppose you have a good friend who lives in a distant city. One day the friend suddenly arrives for a surprise visit. Would it not be queer if, when the friend appeared at your house and called your name, you were to say to him: "Please don't talk to me. I am busy thinking about you"? I think the friend would say, "Think about me when I'm absent! When I'm with you, just be with me, talk

to me." This is the difference between meditation or contemplation (thinking about the Lord and his place in my
life) and real prayer, which is being with the Lord. We could
say that when we begin to use this second way of drawing
water, we are then beginning to learn what prayer really is.
All the labor of "getting to know" begins to bear fruit in the
joy of "being with."

Of course, as in human friendships, the transition is usually gradual. We become really at home with one another
slowly and almost imperceptibly. Moments of ease and moments of awkwardness are interwoven. This is why Teresa's
image is singularly appropriate, and why she says that the
soul "got tired turning the crank, and working with the intellect, and filling the aqueducts." At this time we still go to
the well of meditation or contemplation: we are still discovering who God is for us. But much more time is spent now
in savoring the water which seems often to rise near the surface of the well. And then our thinking, our words get in the
way. At first, as I said, we feel somewhat awkward in this
new relationship. We are so accustomed to doing something
that we feel ill at ease just being still.

Or, even if we are at peace in the stillness of the prayer
of quiet, we find ourselves questioning later whether we
were really praying. People have often said to me: "I am not
sure what is happening. My prayer is peaceful but much
of the time I just seem to be blank." If I ask them, "Are you
restless?" they reply, "Oh, no. While praying I am quite contented and happy. But it seems as if I should be doing something. Sometimes I wonder whether I'm just getting lazy. At
times I'm not even sure whether I was sleeping. I'm afraid
my prayer may be insulting God rather than praising him."
Usually I ask at this point whether the doubts arose while
praying, or only afterward during reflection on the prayer.
And the answer often is "Only afterward. While I was at
prayer I was quite content and peaceful." This is a good sign

that what is happening is genuine prayer. If things seem right when God is close, and our doubts only arise later when we are talking to ourselves, analyzing what happened, then we should not pay much attention to those doubts. It is true that we could just be deceiving ourselves, given our human frailty, and our almost limitless capacity for self-deception. But in this case the difficulty is easily handled. I recommend two things. First, be open to a good director and expect to hear the Lord through him or her. If the director judges that you are on the right path, trust that judgment and proceed in peace. Second, simply say to the Lord, "Lord, you care for me more than I care for myself, and you know my stupidity. You are not playing games with me. So, if I am deceiving myself, you make it clear to me. Until you do, I will trust you and the director and will continue peacefully on the path of stillness."

• • •

Remembering With Joy:
How the Understanding and
the Imagination Help the Will

Teresa attempts to explain what is happening in this way:

> In this prayer the faculties are gathered within so as to enjoy that satisfaction with greater delight. But they are not lost, nor do they sleep. Only the will is occupied in such a way that, without knowing how, it becomes captive; it merely consents to God allowing him to imprison it as one who well knows how to be the captive of its lover. O Jesus and my Lord! How valuable is your love to us here! It holds our love so bound that it doesn't allow it the freedom during that time to love anything else but you.[16]

57

Teresa's language is somewhat obscure here, which is understandable given the obscurity of the experience she is seeking to describe. But her basic idea may be made clear enough.

The faculties to which she refers are the will, the understanding, and the memory or imagination. Normally they are not only intensely active but also quite scattered. Even in the early stages of prayer, when we are learning to meditate with the understanding or contemplate with the imagination, it takes great effort to concentrate them on the subject of our prayer. Gradually we achieve some ability to focus them, although it is always somewhat laborious. But now, when we begin to draw water in the second way with the help of the pump of divine grace, the faculties are easily concentrated, focused, "recollected"—not so much by our efforts as by the work of God. Thus, the will is "captured" by the love of God and finds itself, easily and spontaneously, wholly occupied with God.

What about the other faculties, the understanding and the imagination, which labored so hard when we first went to the well? Teresa says the will alone is occupied, and yet she says the other faculties "are not lost, nor do they sleep."[17] Somehow they are active and involved in our prayer, even though it is the will which is primarily "captured" by God here. This is how Teresa describes the activity of the imagination and the understanding:

> The other two faculties help the will to be capable of enjoying so much good—although sometimes it happens that even though the will is united, they are very unhelpful. But then it shouldn't pay any attention to them; rather it should remain in its joy and quietude. Because if the will desires to gather in these faculties, they both get lost.[18]

Teresa says very little about how the understanding and the imagination "help" the will at this time. But recall how the thought of someone we love stirs our heart. It is now not so much a question of new understanding or insight but rather of "remembering." When my father died in 1973, the family sent a simple memorial card to each of the many friends who consoled us. On it we wrote:

Remember with joy
George C. Green
March 20, 1906–June 7, 1973

"Remember with joy": That short phrase captured for me the whole meaning of my love for my father. In the years since I have often—daily—remembered him: his gentleness, his optimism, his strong faith, his one-note singing voice, what we would call in the Philippines his "Sigurista" nature (much to the exasperation of my mother, he wore both a belt and suspenders, to be secure against the day when the force of gravity might suddenly increase!), his conviction that it would be very difficult for a Democrat, especially a Democratic politician, to reach heaven. Occasionally, even today, I have some new insight into my father's personality and values. But usually it is simply a remembering, a recalling of what I already know and the mind's remembering brings joy to the heart.

It is like that with the Lord. When Jesus was about to die, he was anxious that we remember his love for us, that we remember him. The Eucharist as often as it was celebrated, was to be done "in memory of me." In fact, I believe that we could define a Christian as one who truly remembers the Lord. As one of our most beautiful contemporary songs puts it: "All I ask of you is forever to remember me as loving you." When our prayer becomes more "quiet," when we begin to draw water from the well in this second way, our understanding and our imagination become the organs

59

of remembering the Lord and his love for us. This remembering moves the will to love him, just as my memories of my father touch my heart; this is to "remember with joy." It explains, I believe, what Teresa means by saying that the other two faculties help the will at this time. The labor at the pump is largely the labor (if we can really call it that) of remembering, and it starts the flow of the "waters of joy."

• • •

Distracting Children at an Adult Party

Teresa says, however, that the other faculties, the understanding and the imagination, can actually interfere with the will's work of loving. In fact, she spends most of her time discussing how they do interfere with this work. "But then it shouldn't pay any attention to them; rather it should remain in its joy and quietude. Because if the will desires to gather in these faculties, they both get lost." Teresa compares the understanding and imagination at such a time to "doves that are dissatisfied with the food the owner of the dovecot gives them without their having to work. They go to look for food elsewhere. . . ."[19] What she means is that the understanding and imagination, which before were so active in seeking insights and images which might move the heart, now seem to be "on the sidelines," left out of the work of prayer, or at least having a very small part to play. Since they are very active faculties (constantly at work even when we are sleeping), they find themselves restless in the present situation, where God seems to touch the heart without much help from our thoughts or images.

I have found another metaphor helpful here to clarify the point Teresa is making with her image of the doves.[20] Imagine that you and I are having a serious conversation, perhaps about prayer. And imagine that your small children (or perhaps your nieces and nephews) are present as we talk. Since our conversation about prayer would mean very little to them, they would become restless and begin clamoring for attention. They might start calling your name, pulling at you, demanding attention for themselves. If they were unable to get your attention they would eventually wander off by themselves and, depending on their upbringing and their energy, either proceed to demolish the house or settle down in some corner to play a game by themselves. The point is this: In the prayer of quiet, where God works directly on the will, the understanding and the imagination are like restless children. They seem to be left out of the work of loving which engages the adults (God and the will), and so, like the children, they clamor for attention. This is what we mean by involuntary distractions, which we don't seek or deliberately entertain but which seem to "just come" and sometimes to be very persistent. What should we do about them?

Surprisingly, the best answer is: Just ignore them! Like the children who cannot understand, and are not involved in the adult conversation, our faculties seek something meaningful for themselves. If we are continually trying to control them, to keep them quiet, if the will is continually struggling to subdue the understanding and the imagination, then all its energy will be consumed by this struggle and the will's loving contact with God will be lost. Usually it is best to ignore the wandering imagination and thoughts, unless they become so noisy that the adult conversation is really interrupted, in which case a good spanking or a reprimand is in order. If we ignore them they will gradually settle down. Meanwhile, the adults—the will and God—will be able to share deeply in the encounter of love.

The whole experience is admittedly very mysterious. But I think the analogy of the adults and the children can help us to see what is happening and, more importantly, how we should react. At the beginning of our prayer life, when we are using our own faculties to think about God, the problem is one of concentration, keeping our thoughts focused on the subject of our prayer, not wandering to other topics. At this time we have to exert effort to discipline our mind and imagination, since this is "where the action is."

As our prayer moves from knowing to loving the focus shifts, since it is the will that loves. Now the mind and imagination are no longer where the action is; they are merely assisting the will in its work of loving by their work of remembering, and occasionally enjoying the "overflow" (devout thoughts and images) of the will's love for the Lord. Frequently they are dissatisfied that they are no longer the center of attention—like children at a party when attention shifts from them and their childish concerns to the proper concerns of adults. Like the children they will clamor for attention. If we spend all our time trying to control them, then they have succeeded in keeping attention on themselves. They will know what to do in the future whenever they feel left out by the adults. We will have produced spoiled children, with the whole life of the family centered on their childish concerns.

Now we can see why Teresa gives the advice, at first glance surprising, simply to ignore these distractions at this stage of our prayer life. When they interfere with the will's work of loving, she says that the will "shouldn't pay any attention to them; rather it should remain in its joy and quietude. Because if the will desires to gather in these faculties, they both get lost."[21]

• • •

Streams and Rains: Better Ways of Watering

Fortunately, this second way of drawing water is not the best there is. The pump is a great improvement on the labor of drawing water from the well by hand. But it still involves some labor, with our mind and imagination, and some problems with distractions, which we have been discussing. There is a better way still, and it is this that Teresa describes in the third and fourth ways of drawing water. These ways are purely a gift of God, which we can do nothing to bring about. They normally will come only after many years of a dedicated life of prayer.[22] But a brief discussion of them here will help us to see more clearly the road along which God is leading the soul which desires to be totally given to him.

The third way of drawing the water of prayer for the garden of the Lord is "from a river or a stream. (The garden is watered much better by this means because the ground is more fully soaked, and there is no need to water so frequently—and much less work for the gardener.)" The fourth way is "by a great deal of rain. (For the Lord waters the garden without any work on our part—and this way is incomparably better than all the others mentioned.)" The image is very striking, and the basic progression it seeks to convey is quite clear: At each succeeding stage of the interior journey, God does more and more of the work, and we do less and less. In the beginning, the labor of drawing the water of devotion from the well by hand is very great compared to the yield of water. When the Lord provides the pump (of the prayer of quiet) we still do some work with our faculties (primarily what we called the work of remembering), but much less labor yields much more water. One day, if the Lord so pleases, we find a stream flowing through the garden: the water is there and we have done nothing to secure it. Even our work of remembering seems unnecessary; God comes to us without our doing anything to seek him. We arise in the morning and take up our bucket to go to the pump, and, lo and behold, the water of the Lord's presence is right at our feet.

What must we do now? Only one thing, Teresa says: to "direct" or channel the water to the flowers.[23] The water of prayer is not to be drunk for its own sake, but it is "for the flowers," for the virtues. In terms of her metaphor, it is no good to have a stream flowing through the garden if it just flows in one side and out the other without getting to the roots of the plants. At this stage, where the water appears without any effort on our part, the primary labor of the tenants is irrigation. The water of God's love flows in us without any labor of ours, but we must still cooperate in making this water a source of life for the virtues in the garden of the Lord.

It is probably impossible to explain the experience of the stream flowing through the garden (that God takes over totally the work of prayer) to someone whose heart has not yet experienced it. Even more inexplicable is the fourth way of drawing water, which is not a "drawing" at all since the fourth way is the "rain" of God in which we do nothing, not even channel the rain to the flowers. All we can do now is sit under a tree and let it rain! As I say, there is no way to explain these ways to one who has not yet experienced them. I have read Teresa's chapters XVI to XXII, where she discusses these ways, countless times—and each time I seem to understand them differently, and sometimes I decide I have never really understood them at all! My only consolation is that I suspect Teresa herself might have said the same thing.

Despite the mystery of God's workings, though, the essential point is clear: As we grow, the Lord does more and more of the work and we do less and less. As Teresa says, "The Lord is now pleased to help the gardener, so that he may almost be said to be the gardener himself, for it is he who does everything."[24] This means that, more and more, our prayer becomes the time we give the Lord to shape us, to transform us. The art of praying, as we grow, is really the art of learning to waste time gracefully—to be simply the clay in the hands of the potter. This may sound easy—too easy to be true—but it is really the most difficult thing we ever learn to do. It is much easier to say our novenas, to work for the kingdom, or even to continue to meditate, to keep the control of our destinies in our own hands. As we shall see in part two of this book, this is the real reason why so few of us ever come, in this life, to the full experience of God's love for us.

But for those blessed souls who are able to let go, to float free, a new and mysterious world is revealed. It is a world more mysterious, more exotic and, initially, more threatening than the new world Columbus and Magellan stumbled upon. Those who "stay home" will only know of it by hearsay, and will scarcely believe what they hear. The few whom grace and their own generosity launch on the uncharted sea—they alone will ever really know whether the explorers' tales are true.

2

THE WATER IS

FOR THE FLOWERS

• • •

For the Magellans and the Columbuses of the spiritual life, the quest has begun and the unknown, uncharted seas open before them. But what of their ties to the "folks at home"? When they gather for their shipboard prayers, can they "thank God that they are not like the rest of men and women," earthbound, timid, too cautious, or too attached to cut themselves loose on the open sea? Can they cut their ties, shed their concern for those who remain at home and concentrate all their energies on the journey ahead?

The Christian response is not easy to formulate. An elitist religious tradition can sometimes make a harsh pharisaical judgment on the common herd: Those too worldly to break free and seek God deserve only the contempt of the elite. Even in the early church there seems to have been something of this attitude in many of those who fled to the desert to become hermits. The spirituality of some contemplative, monastic authors is also tinged by this thinking.[1]

It is only in recent years that there has been a real revulsion from this elitist "spirituality of flight." The church has been influenced profoundly by the socialist-Marxist revolution in socio-political thinking. Flight from the world would now appear to be the most irrelevant, anti-gospel choice one could make. We have, rather, a romantic "mystique of the masses," a "massification" of spirituality, a cult of the ordinary. As in art and culture generally, excellence is suspect and "elite" has become a dirty word.

What is the gospel truth? As I said, it is not easy to formulate in one simple, clear-cut phrase. After all, Jesus said some rather strong things which have a definite elitist, anti-worldly sound. It is striking that we read in St. Luke, whose gospel has been known as "the gospel of social concern," these remarkable words:

> As they traveled along, they met a man on the road who said to him, "I will follow you wherever you go." Jesus answered, "Foxes have holes and birds of the air have nests, but the Son of man has nowhere to lay his head." Another to whom he said, "Follow me," replied, "Let me go and bury my father first." But he answered, "Leave the dead to bury their dead; your duty is to go and spread the news of the kingdom of God." Another said, "I will follow you, sir, but first let me go and say good-bye to my people at home." Jesus said to him, "Once the hand is laid to the plough, no one who looks back is fit for the kingdom of God" (Lk 9:57–60).

The first part of this passage has been interpreted (mistakenly, I believe) as canonizing material poverty—that is, as indicating that Jesus is identified with the masses, too poor even to own his own home.[2] But what about the subsequent lines? Is it really human not to care about burying the dead? Or to abandon one's family to the extent of not even saying good-bye to them? Such a spirituality sounds very unworldly, even anti-worldly. This passage, while unusually strong in its demands, is by no means unique in the gospels. The demands of renunciation which Jesus makes of the rich young man are so severe that, when the man goes away sad because of his many possessions, he says, "It is easier for a camel to pass through the eye of a needle than for someone rich to enter the kingdom of Heaven" (Mt 19:24). The disciples are alarmed and ask: "Who can be saved, then?" Jesus' answer is uncompromising: "By human resources, this is impossible; for God everything is possible."

The point is that there seems to be a definite, elitist tinge to Jesus' teaching on discipleship: Being a Christian is not an automatic thing; Christianity is not a mass phenomenon. Jesus makes it quite explicit in chapter 6 of St. John, when first the crowd turned against him because of the faith he demanded (6:41), and then many of his own disciples rejected his further revelation of the eucharist by saying, "This is intolerable language. How could anyone accept it?" (6:60). When he insisted, many of them "went away and accompanied him no more" (6:66). Yet, even when the demands of discipleship drove away his very followers, Jesus did not back down. He simply turned to the Twelve and asked, "Do you want to go away, too?" One can accept the gospel demands or one can freely "go away," but one can never make them more popular, reasonable, palatable, and still follow Jesus Christ. Peter's answer to Jesus reflects the anguish that such a choice creates in the person who is truly drawn to follow him: "Lord, to whom shall we go? You have the message of eternal life" (6:68). Peter finds the demands of Jesus as difficult as any of those who walked with him no longer. He stays with Jesus not because he has found his words reasonable, but because he has found God in him. No wonder Jesus said earlier, "No one can come to me unless drawn by the Father" (6:44).

It all comes down to faith, which the author of Hebrews calls "confident assurance concerning what we hope for, and conviction about things we do not see" (11:1). There is a certain "reasonableness" to faith, in the sense that Peter's "Lord, to whom shall we go?" is reasonable. If he is our only hope, it is foolish, unreasonable, to abandon him. But the demands of faith can never be made reasonable in the sense of palatable, digestible by our human reason and our feelings. Dietrich Bonhoeffer, the German Lutheran pastor put to death by the Nazis, reflecting the influence of Soren Kierkegaard, one of the great masters of the Christian search for faith, has said it beautifully: "When God calls man, he bids him come and die." This line has become one of the mantras of my own interior life, precisely because it captures so beautifully the heart of the gospel call: "If anyone wants to be a follower of mine, let him renounce himself and take up his cross and follow me. Anyone who wants to save his life will lose it; but anyone who loses his life for my sake will find it" (Mt 16:24–25). This saying of Jesus is provoked by Peter's reaction to Jesus' first prophecy of the Passion. Peter objects, "Heaven preserve you, Lord, this must not happen to you!" Jesus replies to Peter: "You are thinking not as God thinks, but as human beings do." The call of God to die is never, either for Jesus or for his disciple, reasonable by human standards.

My point, then, is that Christianity is elitist, but not in the sense that it is only for a chosen few, chosen by reason of race or intelligence or economic standing. It is elitist because it demands real and total commitment to a cross and to death. It is not a mass phenomenon, a cult of mediocrity—and whenever it is lived or preached that way, the good news of Jesus Christ is betrayed. Peter had to learn that lesson painfully ("Get behind me, Satan!"), and so must we.

The Greatest Demand:
Universal and All-Embracing Love

There is, however, another side to the gospel. Marxism is also elitist in its demands on the lives of the elect—the party members. Marxism is also a faith, a secular faith, which can never be made fully reasonable to its followers. Committed Marxists do not believe because they see the ideal embodied in the existing society, but because of their faith that, despite the evidence of corruption and venality and "backsliding" which abounds, the ideal society will evolve by the inexorable laws of history. And yet Marxism and Christianity are diametrically opposed because Christianity has another side. The real conflict, I believe, is not "God vs. no God," but rather love vs. hate. Marxism is grounded in a deterministic view of history, where persons are sacrificed to the ideal state (the "god") and where progress is achieved by conflict between opposing social classes. It is the Darwinian idea of "the survival of the fittest," transposed to human society. The competition, the struggle between persons and social classes is simply nature's way of evolving toward the ideal Marxist society. Progress is achieved by struggle and destruction.[3]

This kind of "progress by hate" has no place in a genuine Christianity. The fundamental demand of Christ is that we love one another, that we love the weak, the crippled, the poor, the rich, that we love even our enemies. Paul's hymn to love in 1 Corinthians 13 is the capstone of his vision of the Christian community, the "better way" which unites all the other virtues. ("Over all these virtues put on love, which binds the rest together and makes them perfect" Col 3:14.) But it is in St. John's Gospel and epistle that the command to "love one another" is given its greatest prominence. In the Last Supper discourse, Jesus stresses that "It is by your love for one another, that everyone will recognize you as my disciples" (Jn 13:35; see also 15:12). It is his "new commandment," on which he insists as the time of his death and departure from them draws near. This is the dominant theme of John's first epistle also, and the climax of John's teaching is the striking statement: "Anyone who says, 'I love God,' and hates his brother, is a liar, since whoever does not love the brother whom he can see cannot love the God whom he has not seen. Indeed, this is the commandment we have received from him, that whoever loves God, must also love his brother" (1 Jn 4:20–21).

In the Sermon on the Mount Jesus extends this love beyond the community of friends and fellow believers:

> *You have heard how it was said, "You will love your neighbor and hate your enemy." But I say this to you, love your enemies and pray for those who persecute you; so that you may be children of your Father in heaven, for he causes his sun to rise on the bad as well as the good, and sends down rain to fall on the upright and the wicked alike. For if you love those who love you, what reward will you get? Do not even the tax collectors do as much? And if you save your greetings for your brothers, are you doing anything exceptional? Do not even the gentiles do as much? You must therefore be perfect, just as your heavenly Father is perfect (Mt 5:43–48).*

This is a hard doctrine, indeed! In fact, as I write these lines I am surprised that Matthew doesn't also tell us here that many of his disciples "walked with him no longer." It is truly difficult to accept the eucharist and the cross, but is it not at least as difficult to accept, and to believe possible, this command to love even our enemies? The thought is exalted and beautiful, but can the Lord seriously expect us to live it?

He does, of course. But there is an important clue in the final sentence of the *New American Bible* rendition of the above quote from the Sermon on the Mount: "You must be made perfect as your heavenly Father is perfect." I doubt whether all scripture scholars would consider this a correct literal rendition of Jesus' words in Matthew ("Be perfect"), but it does convey an important spiritual truth revealed by Jesus: His command to us is not "make yourself perfect," but "be made" perfect. The love, even for our enemies, which Jesus commands is not our work but his work in us. That makes all the difference. As he said after the rich young man departed, "Things that are impossible by human resources are possible to God." (See also Paul's teaching in 1 Corinthians 4:7 and 2 Corinthians 12:9–10). This is the third strand in the rope of gospel spirituality which we have been weaving. First, the elitist demands of faith; second, the universal demands of love for all people. And now—it only occurs to me as I write this—the third strand is hope. It had to be: Hope in the Lord to work in us what we could never accomplish by ourselves—"infinitely more than we ask or imagine" (Eph 3:20).

Paul is the great apostle of hope, of trust, and perhaps no passage in his writings is more beautiful than his hymn of hope in Romans 8. The desperate situation he describes in Romans 7—torn apart by the "two laws" that war within him—leads to the triumphant affirmation of 8:1: "Condemnation will never come for those who are in Christ Jesus!" This leads to the beautiful panoramic view of a redeemed world in which the Spirit of Jesus dwells in us (8:9), leads us to God (8:14), testifies to our divine adoption (8:16), even prays in us when we do not know how to pray "with groans which cannot be put into words" (8:26). With all this, Paul exclaims, what more can we ask? "If God is for us, who can be against us?" (8:31). To live the gospel demands of faith and love is impossible to us by our own strength. But all things are possible to God, and his gift to us of his Spirit is the pledge, the guarantee of his unconditioned fidelity. "If we are unfaithful he will still remain faithful, for he cannot deny himself."[4] Thus the fidelity of God, and not any virtue we see in ourselves, is the only sure basis for our living the life of faith and love to which the gospel calls us.

• • •

The Tension of Total Commitment and Involvement

We began this chapter by asking about the worldly ties of those who, like Columbus and Magellan, have begun a journey into the unknown. Here the journey is the life of prayer; the "mysterious East" toward which we are drawn is the great God himself. Does such a drawing mean a leaving behind, a losing interest in the world from which we came? The answer which the scriptures have given us is a qualified "no." That is, any spirituality which neglects the demands of fraternal love and concern—even the demands of love for one's enemies—cannot be authentically Christian. And yet, as I said, the answer is a qualified "no," because it is true that the demands of faith do alienate us from the values and thinking of the world in which we live. We are "in the world but not of the world," to put it as Jesus does at the Last Supper (Jn 17:11, 14–16): we are not to be taken out of the world, and yet we do not belong to the world any more than Jesus himself did. We live in a situation of tension as long as this present life lasts, a tension which only increases as we draw closer to God. Moreover, as we have seen, this tension is creative and not destructive only if we live in hope—hope in the fidelity of God as the pledge of our fidelity to him in this ambivalent situation.

But why, you might ask, does this question about our relationship to the world now arise? Why do we devote so much time to it? The reason is because one who begins to experience the prayer of quiet (Teresa's second way of drawing water) is very likely to experience this tension. Within the past month alone, at the time I write these pages, at least ten active apostles—priests, sisters, seminarians—have put this question to me. They have tested the waters of God, and the question arises whether perhaps they are called to give their whole lives to prayer. I have concluded, from my experience as a director, that this question almost inevitably arises for any genuinely mature person of prayer. The pull of God is so strong; am I perhaps called to give my whole life to the exclusive pursuit of him in a contemplative community?

I have had to face the same question myself. During my years of Jesuit formation God became more and more the center of my being. When I first entered the novitiate I was, at best, a reluctant friend of the Lord. A good schooling and a good home had given me a basic religious sense and a certain piety, but the Lord was just one of many people to whom I was attached. I also had my parents, my friends, a girlfriend—and I had no desire for the Lord to get a total hold on my heart. That he should be first, yes, but first among equals! When, in the early days of novitiate, I sensed that the Lord wanted something more than that, I was anxious to get out of the novitiate before I was trapped! But I wanted to prove to myself that I did not really have a vocation, that it was really the Lord's will that I not be trapped by him.

Fortunately, I had a novice master who knew how to handle the situation. He was a man I feared and felt ill at ease with. (Even today, if I met him I am sure I would feel the impulse to uncross my legs and sit up straight in my chair!) But he handled me perfectly in this situation and for that I shall be, quite literally, eternally grateful to him. When I told him my reasons why I did not have a vocation, he considered them for a day and then told me: "It seems clear to me you do have a vocation. You are perfectly free to leave the novitiate right now; but at least be honest enough to admit to yourself that you are leaving not because you don't have a vocation, but because you are not generous enough to accept it." That was a great blow to my pride (it is ironic to think that I am still a Jesuit today because of that pride!) and I could not admit it. But in the following months, while I was trying to convince him and myself I did not have a vocation, something happened. Without really wanting it, I began to fall in love with the Lord and woke up one day to realize I really did want to stay. I was trapped and was happy to be trapped. And in the years that followed, despite all the usual ups and downs and infidelities, that centering on the Lord continued to grow in me.

Then one day—I don't recall when—the question came whether the Lord was calling me to the contemplative life. Was that the real meaning, the logical outcome of the drawing of his love which I experienced? It is the same question many other friends of God have put to me in the years since. Can we only truly draw deeply from the well of God if we renounce the world and give ourselves wholly to him in a cloistered life, secluded from the world?

• • •

Contemplative Prayer vs. Life in a Contemplative Community

The answer to my own personal question came in a surprising place. About 1970, when I was finishing my graduate studies, I made my annual retreat at the Trappist monastery of Our Lady of the Genesee, near my home in Rochester. The retreat was something I had long dreamed of, and it fulfilled all my expectations. God was very close. The setting and the monastic routine provided an ideal climate for prayer. Yet, surprisingly, it then became very clear to me—so clear that the conviction has lasted to this day—that the Lord was not calling me to the monastic life. I saw the cloistered contemplative life as a legitimate and even necessary part of the total life of the church. But it was not his call to me.

Why? At the time this was not so clear to me. In the years that followed, however, I began to realize two very important things. The first was that there is a real difference between a call to a life of contemplative prayer and a call to life in a contemplative community. The call to contemplative prayer—that is, to prayer in which we do less and less and God does more and more, to an experience of God which is not primarily the result of our own labor at the well of meditation, but is more and more the mysterious free gift of God—this call is given to many, perhaps most, of those who seriously seek the Lord.[5] Yet, at the same time they are called to live "in the world." The somewhat rare call to life in a contemplative community seems to be a sacrament, a sign and a reminder to the church of the universal call of all men and women to know God in prayer: "This is eternal life, to know you, the one true God, and him whom you have sent, Jesus Christ" (Jn 17:3). Eternal life is "to know God." The call to contemplative prayer, to Teresa's second way of drawing water, is the Lord's invitation to begin eternal life now and not to wait until we die. This invitation is the heart and meaning of the vocation of Mary, of those called to life in a "contemplative" community. But, in his goodness, the invitation is also given to many who are Martha, and they are faced with the much more challenging task of being both Mary and Martha in one life: of being "busy about many things" for the sake of the Lord and yet at the same time allowing their lives to be centered on the "one thing necessary" which Mary had found (Lk 10:38–42).[6]

There are, then, not only Marys and Marthas in the church, but also Martha-Marys. In fact, I would suspect that Martha has little chance of being truly happy in the home of the Lord unless she discovers that her middle name is Mary. This leads us to the second realization (the central point of this chapter) which has come to me in the years since my Trappist retreat. Briefly put, it is this: the water is for the flowers. The joy of experiencing God in prayer is not an end in itself, but is the water by which the virtues are strengthened and brought to full flowering. When Peter saw the Lord transfigured on the holy mountain, he could not build three tents there, remain forever, and forget the rest of the apostles. And when Magdalene met the Lord in the garden on Easter morning, she could not cling to him forever. She had to return to the city, to the center of her life, to share with the disciples the Lord she had found (Mk 9:2–13 and Jn 20:11–18, respectively). Peter's and Magdalene's experiences of the Lord had to lead to action, had to make some differences in their own lives and in the life of the church.

• • •

Seek the Flowers, Not the Water

It is the same with us. No matter how beautiful and moving our experience of God in prayer may be, it must always be suspect if it does not lead to good results in our lives. Teresa makes the same point frequently in her discussion of the four ways of drawing water. This is significant since Teresa herself was the foundress of a reformed community of cloistered contemplative nuns. We would tend to think that the cloistered life means giving one's whole time to prayer. Not Teresa. She insists that even for contemplatives the water is for the flowers. She is, in fact, very suspicious of a prayer life which is too centered on itself. She advises superiors at one point that, if they have a sister who is experiencing visions and other unusual phenomena, they should give her extra work in the kitchen! That, says Teresa, will take care of most visions!

One of my favorite passages in Teresa's writings is in the Fourth Mansions of the *Interior Castle*. In this work, written some fourteen years after she completed her *Autobiography*, Teresa compares the soul to a castle—an interior castle—in which there are many mansions. The interior life is a journey inward, from the outermost mansions where most people dwell to the very center of our being, the Seventh Mansions, where God dwells. The Fourth Mansions, as Teresa herself indicates, corresponds to the second way of drawing water, the beginning of our properly supernatural encounter with God.[7] In that context she says: "If you would progress a long way on this road and ascend to the mansions of your desire, the important thing is not to think much, but to love much; do, then, whatever most arouses you to love." We have seen this point already in the move from the first way of drawing water to the second: prayer is not thinking but loving, and meditation must give way to "being with." But Teresa has more than this in mind. She continues: "Perhaps we do not know what love is: it would not surprise me a great deal to learn this, for love consists, not in the extent of our happiness, but in the firmness of our determination to try to please God in everything, and to endeavor, in all possible ways, not to offend him, and to pray him ever to advance the honor and glory of his son and the growth of the Catholic Church. Those are the signs of love."[8] In other words, the fruits of genuine prayer are not so much in the consoling quality of the prayer itself but in our lives.

Teresa is totally in harmony with the teaching of scripture as we saw it in the early pages of this chapter. The genuine life of prayer is marked by growth in faith, in hope, and in love: a faith which is not merely words but a lived acceptance of the cross, the eucharist, and of Jesus' whole way of seeing the world; a hope grounded in our experience of God which enables us to believe in the Lord's victory in us and in the world even in the face of human defeat and disaster; and a love which sees all things and all people, even our "enemies," with the eyes of God and treats them accordingly. These, in summary, are the flowers in the garden of the Lord. The water of prayer is for them. If they are thriving and blooming our prayer life is quite genuine—even if there seems to be no water at all.

• • •

Virtues Natural and Graced

Can we be sure? Could it be that these virtues are merely natural, the result either of a naturally good temperament, of a good upbringing, or of a humanistic training such as Confucius or the Stoics propound so beautifully? I think it is true that much of what we call virtue can be explained naturally. In fact, in religious communities we often confuse this natural goodness with holiness. This is why I find that my judgments of people, as a director, often vary from the external judgments that members of the community make of one another. In fact, my judgments of people often change radically once they share with me their inner lives. Some people are naturally cheerful, pliable, energetic, service-oriented. And others are naturally worrisome, stubborn (oftentimes a survival mechanism for those of limited intelligence or opportunity), lethargic, hesitant to get involved. It is very tempting to categorize the first group as holy and the second group as spiritually mediocre.

Both judgments could easily be mistaken. Let us consider each separately. The virtuous or holy who are such merely because of temperament or environment are not necessarily holy at all. The virtues about which Teresa is speaking, and about which the gospel speaks, are not of this

79

type. No one naturally finds the cross reasonable or desirable; the faith which embraces the cross is not masochism. Rather, it is a desire, despite a shrinking from the human suffering involved (Gethsemane), to be totally one with the one I love. No one naturally hopes for victory in the very face of helplessness and defeat.[9] There is really no Christian hope except in the very face of human helplessness and defeat; this is very different from the Pollyanna attitude of one who closes his or her eyes to the real situation. Finally, no one naturally loves his enemies. That, as Jesus has said, is precisely what distinguishes the Christian from the good pagan. People who like everybody naturally are very comfortable to be with, but almost certainly they have no depth; they don't care passionately about anything or anybody. If they like everyone, there is a good possibility they don't love anyone.

Fortunately, Jesus did not command us to like all people, not even our enemies. That command would be impossible for us to fulfill without a real miracle of grace—a miracle which in my experience is very rare, since our "likes" are rooted in our instincts and feelings. These are usually the last part of us to be healed by grace. He did command us to love even those we don't like, that is, sincerely to desire their good. This, too, is not naturally possible, but it is the fruit of a genuine love of the Lord, and it is manifested in the lives of good Christians even though their likes and dislikes persist.

My point, then, is that it is not the natural qualities of temperament and upbringing which are the marks of a genuine and solid spirituality. It is rather those qualities, those virtues (like a love of the cross) which transcend the natural and cannot be explained by any merely human formation. Similarly—to turn to the second group of people mentioned above—the lack of natural virtues is not necessarily a sign of a faulty spirituality. Let me give an example which the person in question has permitted me to share and which is actually typical of several experiences I have had.

• • •

Hope for Difficult Personalities

Some years ago a sister who was evidently a very strong personality asked me to be her spiritual director. As we shared I became more and more aware of her domineering temperament, and yet at the same time of her sincere desire to be truly given to the Lord. (At the beginning, I think, she tried to dominate him, too!) He made it clear to her, with a few helpful hints from me, that this could not be. She found herself more and more willing to surrender to him and to let him be the boss. It was a hard fight! At one point her superior (not knowing, of course, or having any right to know what Sister X and I had shared, but knowing I was her director) said to me: "You have said in your conferences to the community that the fruit of a good interior life is growth in the virtues. How can Sister X have a genuine prayer life when she is so difficult in community? Would this not imply that something is wrong with her prayer?" At first sight the answer would seem to be a clear "Yes"; and yet I was not so sure. I find, as a director, that such situations are very tricky to handle, since the absolute confidentiality of the direction situation must be respected. I usually respond by asking a question of the superior (e.g., "What precisely makes you feel Sister X is so difficult in community?"), and thus restrict the discussion to what the person now sitting in front of me knows and wishes to share. In this case I asked further whether there had been any improvement over the past year or two, and the superior said there had been definite improvement, but certainly not total change. Sister X could still be quite overbearing, demanding, insensitive to others—obviously not good symptoms. And yet I made an interior judgment, admittedly hesitant and tentative, that Sister X was probably genuinely prayerful and on the right path to God.

What made me think so? Such judgments of a director are often "intuitive" (analogous to a doctor's, they depend much on one's total experience as a director) and they depend much on one's own prayerful discernment of how the Lord is working in a given situation. As such they are difficult to rationalize. But I think I can indicate certain factors that were good "signs" in the given case. First of all, Sister X seemed to have been very open to me and quite candid. She saw things from her own point of view, of course, but the picture the superior gave me of the community life did not essentially differ from the picture I already had from Sister X. Secondly, I was able to be quite frank with Sister X, and she accepted this frankness humbly and with grace; moreover, the Lord seemed to be equally frank with her in her prayer, as she shared it with me. Thirdly, and perhaps most importantly, when external difficulties and frustrations arose, she was able to see them and accept them (though not without much frustration and occasional bouts of self-pity) as precisely what she needed to be purified, to be "tamed." There was a final sign which may seem small but which I have come to value highly as a director: When Sister X and I talked, she focused on her own life, her own failings, the ways I could help her to grow. She was not like the person who confesses everybody else's sins—the spouse's, the children's—in the process of ostensibly confessing one's own. To me this is a very good sign of sincerity and of a solidly based spirituality.[10]

Thus, a lack of ease in natural virtue is not necessarily a sign of an inauthentic spirituality. If there are underlying signs of growing faith, hope, and love I would judge that the Spirit of God is at work, even though there are still many thorny (and highly visible) weeds in the garden of the Lord.

After all, he himself told a parable about leaving the weeds to grow with the wheat until the harvest, lest in uprooting the weeds prematurely the fragile shoots of wheat also be uprooted (Mt 13:24–30).[11] I see the same thing in myself. Failings of personality and instinct which I would judge most inconsistent in a man of God seem to persist over the years, despite the fact that the Lord is drawing me closer and closer to him. At times it can be very discouraging and even leads me to question the reality of my prayer life. But deep down, and in my better moments, I know the answer for me is the same as that I have given to the many "Sister Xs" whom I have directed: Instinctual failings and flaws of personality are not necessarily or automatically uprooted by a genuine spirituality. Paul seems to have remained impatient, Teresa domineering, for most if not all of their lives. If there is no growth at all in these areas, the spirituality in question is indeed suspect. But the touchstone virtues of which Teresa speaks are deeper and more faith-centered. It seems, in fact, that our instincts are the last part of us to hear the good news of salvation!

In summary, then, a genuine prayer life, whether lived in the cloister or in the world, is clearly manifested by the difference it makes in our lives. Prayer—the consolation of prayer—is not an end in itself, just as we do not go to the well for water just for the sheer joy of drawing water. The water is for the plants in the garden; prayer is for the virtues. The primary virtues are those which are rooted in and manifest faith, hope, and love. The natural virtues are also part of the garden and they, too, should benefit from the water of prayer. But often they are late-blooming plants in the garden of the Lord, their roots intertwined with many weeds. Eventually the weeds must go and the natural virtues must bloom, but the Lord seems to find delight in a garden with many weeds, provided faith, hope, and love are planted there. It is strange that it is so; I have often thought that if I were God I would never tolerate as weedy a garden as I myself am. But then I thank the Lord that he is God and not I!

• • •

"Much-Afraid" Becomes "Grace and Glory"

Perhaps our point about the water being for the flowers has been best expressed by Hannah Hurnard. In the great allegorical tradition of C. S. Lewis, she has described the journey of the soul to God in terms of a fairy tale, which she calls *Hind's Feet on High Places*.[12] The heroine is named Much-Afraid, and she lives in the Valley of Humiliation, a member of the Fearing family. It is

> the story of how Much-Afraid escaped from her
> Fearing relatives and went with the Shepherd
> to the High Places where "perfect love casteth
> out fear." For several years Much-Afraid had
> been in the service of the Chief Shepherd, whose
> great flocks were pastured down in the Valley of
> Humiliation . . . but happy as she was in most
> ways, she was conscious of several things which
> hindered her in her work and caused her much
> secret distress and shame.[13]

She was a cripple and had a twisted mouth "which greatly disfigured both expression and speech," and was painfully aware of how much these deformities impeded her work and gave people a bad impression of the Chief Shepherd for whom she worked.

The allegory is clear enough to anyone who has come to realize the goodness and holiness of Christ, the "Chief Shepherd," and what a pathetic image of him we, his followers, convey to the world, which judges him by what they see in us. Hind's Feet is the story of Much-Afraid's healing on a journey to the "high places" of the interior life where God dwells. It is a long and arduous journey, but at the end Much-Afraid receives a new name, Grace and Glory, which symbolizes the wondrous transformation the Shepherd has worked in her during her journey.

When I first read Hind's Feet, I was much moved by it. It seemed clear that it was written by someone who had truly experienced the ways of God in prayer, so accurate was the description of what John of the Cross calls the ascent of Mount Carmel. But one thing troubled me: the whole story seemed too inward-looking, too much an only-me-and-Jesus spirituality. Much-Afraid escaped the Valley of Humiliation and discovered her own real self in the love of the Shepherd. But what about those she left behind? Was the valley merely to be escaped from and then forgotten forever? That seemed to contradict the gospel spirituality of Jesus.

This troubled me, because otherwise the book seemed to be a beautiful and accurate description of the interior journey of the soul. How happy I was, then, when I discovered there was a sequel to Hind's Feet, and that the whole point of the sequel was Much-Afraid's return to the Valley of Humiliation—her necessary return, sent by the Chief Shepherd—that others might share the transformation which the Shepherd had worked in her. The sequel is entitled *Mountains of Spices*.[14] It is the story of Much-Afraid's work in the valley from which she came, and the way her own transformation in Christ radiates light into the dark corners of her fearful world. Now the story was complete and completely true to the gospel: Only by giving away what she had found could Much-Afraid keep it; only by dying in turn for the brethren—as the Shepherd had died for her—could she live.

Recently I discovered another and very different kind of book by Hannah Hurnard. It is entitled *Wayfarer in the*

Land[15] and is the story of her work as a Protestant missionary in Palestine in the 1930s and 1940s. The mission was
originally to the Jews, but as time passed Hannah Hurnard
herself felt strongly called to preach also to the Arabic towns
of Palestine—a very risky call for a woman in those days.
At one point she had to transport to a Nazareth hospital
an Arabic woman who had just given birth. En route the
woman died, and the husband who was with them in the
car was beside himself with grief. Hannah Hurnard was
overwhelmed with the tragedy of the situation and her own
helplessness—to save the woman's life and even more to
bring her the good news of Christ before she died. And in
her misery the Lord seemed to say to her: "Grace ('Hannah'
means 'grace'), cannot you trust her to me and my love?
Will you not believe that nothing has been left undone, nor
will be left undone, that can help her? Trust her to me."

This led Hannah to a reflection and an insight which can
very well stand as a summary of this chapter.

> *This experience made a lasting impression on me.
> It was not that I felt afterwards that it did not
> matter so much if we did not urgently seek the
> lost before they left this world, for in the end all
> will be well. Rather it was an overwhelming sense
> of our Lord's passionate love and longing for the
> souls whom he has created, and his determination
> to seek them at all costs, and his longing that we
> should cooperate with him in this work. The one
> thing we cannot do, we who have tasted of his
> love and grace, and been lifted out of the darkness
> and brought into all the joy and power of know-
> ing him, is to sit back comfortably and leave him
> alone in his task of searching for the lost.*[16]

Hannah Hurnard and Teresa of Avila are kindred spirits. Anyone who has come to know the God they know inevitably comes to the same realization: the water is for the flowers. The experience of God, which is the "water of joy," must always, if it is genuine, fructify in the love of God and the love of his children. At the same time, the whole work is really God's. He is the gardener; he plants the flowers; he provides the water; and eventually he makes the well run dry. When this happens, we see it as failure, but God sees it very differently!

3

WHEN THE

WELL RUNS DRY

• • •

When Much-Afraid begins her journey to the high places she is given two silent companions who will be with her until the end. Their names are Sorrow and Suffering, and Much-Afraid recoils from them. She is already "much-afraid"; it seems a cruel trick of the Shepherd to give her, such a timid soul, two such somber companions.[1] Does he really intend to discourage her, to frighten her away from the journey? It seems so to Much-Afraid, and she complains bitterly to her Shepherd. But as time passes she grows to love them, and by the end of the journey she realizes that no one but they could have accompanied her safely to the High Places.

What Much-Afraid learned, everyone who is faithful to prayer must learn too. Like her, we complain bitterly at first. We have read countless times the words of Jesus: "If anyone wants to be a follower of mine, let him renounce himself and take up his cross, and follow me. Anyone who wants to save his life will lose it, but anyone who loses his life for my sake will find it" (Mt 16:24–25). We know that, when he himself came to die, he told Philip and Andrew: "In all truth I tell you, unless a grain of wheat falls into the earth and dies, it remains only a single grain; but if it dies, it yields a rich harvest. Anyone who loves his life loses it, anyone who hates his life in this world will keep it for eternal life" (Jn 12:24–25). We know Jesus spoke this way, but we don't really believe him. Or, if our heads assent to his words, our hearts can't accept them—at least not right now. We are like young people who know very well in their heads that, like all people, they will one day die. That day is so far away that it hardly touches them. It is tomorrow and not today, and tomorrow is unreal. How well I recall the time, just about when I turned forty, when my own mortality began to haunt me. My father was dying, and that may well have triggered the realization that I, too, despite the absence of symptoms of illness, was dying day by day. I don't know, because the thought was not conscious and deliberate. In fact, I was anxious to dismiss it, but it obsessed me. After a year or so it passed, and since then I have been at peace again. But I am not really the same as before: I had to look death in the eye during that year, to accept it as real for me, to "affirm" that my dying was the most real and the single most important event of my life. All of us must die; to accept death, however, to affirm it, to say "yes" to it as the necessary culmination of life, is perhaps the most important and difficult confrontation of a person's life. We then know what Gethsemane really means.

• • •

The Heart of the Matter

For the one who prays, there is an inner dying and an outer dying. We said something in chapter 2 about the outer dying, which takes place gradually in the external events and situations of our lives and only culminates in bodily death. But there is also an inner dying, a dying which takes place in our interior lives, about which we must also speak. It is this inner dying which is the soul of the outer dying of the Christian. It, too, begins early and happens gradually. In Teresa's metaphor of the ways of drawing water, it begins at the time when the well runs dry. As with bodily death, at first it seems disastrous—a loss of God. Only gradually, and with good direction, do we realize that drought means growth.

This inner dying begins very early in the interior life. When St. Teresa is discussing the first way of drawing water, the way of meditation and imaginative contemplation, she has this curious remark, a harbinger of things to come:

> These things make up the beginning of fetching water from the well, and please God that it may be found. At least we are doing our part, for we are already drawing it out and doing what we can to water these flowers. God is so good that when for reasons His Majesty knows—perhaps for our greater benefit—the well is dry and we, like good gardeners, do what lies in our power, he sustains the garden without water and makes the virtues grow.[2]

What should we do if our meditative prayer is "dry," if it does not seem to touch our hearts or lead to the water of consolation? Teresa's answer is very commonsensical: We should look at the flowers, the virtues, and see how they are doing. After all, the water is for the flowers; devotion, as we have seen, is not the goal of a good prayer life—it is a means to the growth of the virtues. If the virtues are alive and flourishing in us, even in the absence of devotion or consolation, then our prayer life is healthy despite the dryness.

On paper this may appear simple and even obvious, at least in the light of all we have said in chapter 2. But in practice it is not at all easy to grasp. We want to see some tangible result of our efforts in prayer, and the result we look for is the water of devotion. Today, especially, we are not satisfied with a prayer that is merely "in the head"; we seek the experience of God, a tangible sense of his presence. Thus far we are right. Meditation and contemplation are not prayer, they are normally a necessary preliminary to prayer: They are the "getting to know" the Lord which makes prayer possible. Prayer is the loving that flows from a deeper and deeper knowing.

As I said, this desire to experience God, to get beyond merely knowing about him to truly loving him, is of the very essence of genuine prayer. That is why Part One of this book is entitled "From Knowing to Loving." In terms of Teresa's metaphor, the labor of lowering the bucket into the well and drawing it up (i.e., meditation and imaginative contemplation) is not for its own sake but for the sake of the water of devotion, of the experience of God. When, in the second way of drawing water, the Lord provides a pump by which we draw the water of the experience of God with much less meditative labor, we do not feel guilty that we are laboring less. Rather, we rejoice in the abundance of water and forget about the excess labor of the past. We feel that now we have truly learned to pray.

How will we feel, then, if the well runs dry? The fact that we are unable to meditate or contemplate will not much bother us as long as the water is flowing freely. In fact, once we realize what is happening, we are quite happy to relax and let the waters of joy flow. But if the waters suddenly stop flowing, we are likely to panic. How have I failed? Why is God so far away? Where have I displeased him? This dryness can be due to our own negligence, our own infidelities. The deeper our love becomes (as is true in human love, too), the more important complete sincerity, complete purity of heart, becomes. This is why the examination of conscience and the sacrament of penance (see chapter 5 of *Opening to God*) are an essential part of even a mature spirituality.

• • •

When We Are Not Negligent

But there can be another explanation for the dryness of the well, for our loss of devotion. Suppose I examine my conscience and find that there are, indeed, many infidelities in my life (as there will always be). Yet, these are the same infidelities I saw in myself last month and last year, and God was very close then. As far as I can see, I am respond-ing the same as then, but now God seems far away. In this case my infidelities are not the reason for the dryness. You might say to me, as many people have said, "Yes, but maybe I am offending God in some way that I don't realize. Maybe he is displeased with something I have done and I don't see what it is." This sounds reasonable, but it is actually impos-sible. I have sometimes said to people: "If that is the kind of God we have, one who is playing guessing games with us, then we don't need a God!" Sometimes we do that: We say to a friend that he has hurt us, and when he asks how he has offended us we say: "That is for you to figure out!" Such behavior is cruel and childish, the mark of a very im-mature person. We might act that way, but the God of love whom Jesus has revealed to us never does. The answer to vague doubts about whether we have offended God is sim-ply to say: "Lord, you care for me more than I care for my-self. I cannot believe that you are playing guessing games with me. If the dryness I experience is due to some failing of mine, you make it clear to me, and I will try to remedy it. But I will not entertain vague doubts; unless and until you make my failing clear to me, I will assume that is not the reason for the dryness." That is a prayer certain to please the God of love, one which he will surely answer!

Fortunately, the Lord works gradually and never tests us beyond our strength. Even fairly early in our interior life there may be periods of dryness not due to our own negligence. Sometimes they will be prolonged. Teresa notes this in talking about the first way of drawing water. She says: "What, then, will he do here who finds that for many days he experiences nothing but aridity, dislike, distaste, and so little desire to go and draw water?" This happens to everyone who prays, and many give up prayer when this happens, especially if they do not have a director to whom they can be open about their experience. This is a tragedy. For one who is properly guided and properly motivated, the experience of aridity that Teresa describes is such

> that if he doesn't recall that doing so serves and gives pleasure to the Lord of the garden, and if he isn't careful to preserve the merits acquired in this service (and even what he hopes to gain from the tedious work of often letting the pail down into the well and pulling it back up without any water), he will abandon everything. It will frequently happen to him that he will even be unable to lift his arms for this work and unable to get a good thought. . . . But, as I am saying, what will the gardener do here? He will rejoice and be consoled and consider it the greatest favor to be able to work in the garden of so great an Emperor![3]

This would certainly not be the natural, spontaneous reaction of the beginner confronted with many days of aridity and distaste in her prayer! Teresa, who is the most practical of women, knows this very well. She is speaking as a director here, telling us how we should act in a very frustrating situation. She goes on to advise the person confronted with this initial experience of desolating dryness:

> *Since he knows that this pleases the Lord and his intention must be not to please himself but to please the Lord, he gives the Lord much praise. For the Master has confidence in the gardener because he sees that without any pay he is so very careful about what he was told to do. This gardener helps Christ carry the cross and reflects that the Lord lived with it all during his life. He doesn't desire the Lord's kingdom here below or ever abandon prayer. And so he is determined, even though this dryness may last for his whole life, not to let Christ fall with the cross.*

• • •

To Share Jesus' Sufferings

Once the beginner, filled with self-pity because of her dryness, hears Teresa's words, she is ashamed of her selfishness. To grasp the full meaning of Teresa's advice takes many years, but even a beginner can sense that there is something wrong when she professes to follow a crucified Lord and yet is discouraged by a few days of dryness. How can my Lord hang on a cross and I be content with a life of sweetness and light? This is the central point Teresa is making: If it is really the God and Father of Jesus Christ whom we are seeking in our prayer, then we must expect to find him as Jesus found him. The author of the epistle to the Hebrews tells us what that means:

> *During his life on earth, he offered up prayer and entreaty, with loud cries and with tears, to the one who had the power to save him from death,*

> *and, winning a hearing by his reverence, he learnt*
> *obedience, Son though he was, through his suffer-*
> *ings; when he had been perfected, he became for*
> *all who obey him the source of eternal salvation*
> *(Heb 5:7–9).*

Jesus "learnt obedience . . . through his suffering" and we are saved by obeying him. No one comes to the Father except through him. He is the way—the only way—to God (Jn 14:6).

St. Paul realized clearly that this means much more than just that Jesus is our guide on a painless path to God. He is not a guide, a pioneer, who has cleared the way so that we can follow to the scenic heights of God like tourists in an air-conditioned bus on a concrete highway. Perhaps it would be nice if that were our situation. (Beginners might think so!) But as we grow we begin to realize that this cannot be the way of love. Pampered tourists have no love for the trailblazers who cleared the way. They may have occasional thoughts of gratitude and wonder, but no love. So it is that St. Paul makes the extraordinary statement which grounds all that Teresa has said about the cross and the person devoted to prayer: "Even now I find my joy in the suffering I endure for you. In my own flesh I fill up what is lacking in the sufferings of Christ for the sake of his body, the church" (Col 1:24). The statement is remarkable: How could anything be lacking to the sufferings of Christ?

Clearly, he could have done it all for us. In fact, he could easily have saved us without dying. Yet, when the Father showed him the way of death, he accepted it totally and lived it perfectly. One of my joys is the realization, when I look at Calvary and at my own flawed love, that in Jesus at least one person loved God perfectly, as I would wish to love him. What, then, can Paul mean by "filling up what is lacking to the sufferings of Christ"? It can only mean that Jesus chose to leave his saving suffering incomplete, in order that we might participate in our own work of redemption by the continuation of the mystery of Calvary in us, in our own flesh. This is the greatest love he could have shown us, to ask us to be partners in our own redemption. Faced with this realization, Teresa asks, how can we want to avoid the cross in our own lives? "This gardener helps Christ carry the cross and reflects that the Lord lived with it all during his life. . . . And so he is determined, even though this dryness may last for his whole life, not to let Christ fall with the cross." This is not just a pious anachronism on Teresa's part, an imaginative re-creation of an event long since finished. She has realized, as Paul did, the deep mystical meaning of our identification with Jesus.

Our experience of dryness in prayer, then, is not merely a frustrating experience of the absence of God. It is an essential experience of our identification with Jesus, who "learned obedience through suffering." More concretely still, the Lord allows it so that we may "learn obedience through suffering," that we may acquire that "passion for God" of which Kierkegaard speaks, that passion for the Father's will which possesses Jesus in St. John's gospel.[4]

In the passage we quoted at length, Teresa is speaking to beginners. I doubt, however, that real beginners, still learning to draw water in the first way (meditation and imaginative contemplation), would really find much meaning in her words. Their problem tends to be more with concentration, with focusing their scattered thoughts on the gospel passage they are meditating on, even with understanding just what prayer is all about. I doubt that this discussion of the importance of dryness would have much meaning for those who were just beginning to learn to pray.[5] It is good, though, that beginners hear of the cross as the heart of the following of Christ right from the very start of their prayer life. They may not understand it, just as the apostles did not understand Jesus' repeated prophecies of the passion. Despite all Jesus had said, they were not prepared for Calvary when it came. But later they will understand, when the Spirit comes to remind them of all they have heard. I often say something similar to seminarians: "What I say to you may not make much sense now, but store it away in your subconscious and the time will come when it will make sense. When you need it you will be able to remember that you did hear it once."

• • •

Courtship and the Cost of Total Commitment

The time when dryness becomes a real concern is usually after our prayer has moved from the head to the heart and we have drunk with joy of the waters of salvation. This first breakthrough in our prayer life—from head to heart—is often followed by some months or years when God is very close and our prayer is joy. There will be peaks and troughs, good and bad days, but generally we can explain them by our own fidelity and infidelity. If prayer is dry, we know that we have been negligent or half-hearted. But when we are faithful God seems only too ready to encounter us in love. This is the time of "courtship," when God is seeking to win us to himself. He makes himself competitive with the other possible loves which attract us: family, career and (especially for men)[6] our own independence. We know the joy of his presence, but we hesitate to commit ourselves wholeheartedly. Like Francis Thompson, we fear "lest having him, we might have naught besides." Our fervor easily cools when we think of, and are present to, the other goods which attract us. The carefree bachelor finally falling in love with a girl is confronted with the same dilemma; it is a joy to be with her, but the cost of total commitment seems too great. What of his independence, his nights out with the boys, his freedom to do whatever he would like and not have to worry about what she would like? So, too, the one who is beginning to taste the waters of God is caught in a dilemma. To love means to live for another. We are afraid that, as one of the seminarians put it to me, "If I find God, I may lose Tom." If only the Lord would be satisfied with just being one of the "boys"!

But, of course, he is not satisfied with this. At this time of "courtship" he seems to respond eagerly whenever we seek him. Yet, our infidelities, and the spiritual dryness they produce, are continually present to haunt us and to remind us of the schizophrenic life we are leading. We become more and more dissatisfied with our hesitancy to commit ourselves. The very consolations which God gives us simply increase our dissatisfaction with our own on-and-off response. One day, perhaps during a retreat, we finally face ourselves and the demands of love. We face the fact that sooner or later our commitment to the Lord must be all or nothing. It is a painful moment, but a moment of great grace. It is the moment of truth which the rich young man experienced when he came face to face with the Lord. If we survive the crisis and are able, by God's grace, to really say "Yes!" to love, it is a crucial turning point in our lives. Prayer becomes not just something we do, one thing among others, but the very air we breathe. The Lord is no longer just one of the "boys." He has become the very center of our lives. We may—we will—still fail. There will be times, as we face the demands of growth, when we are tempted to hold back or even to break our commitment, but deep down we know to whom our heart belongs.

What happens now? Surprisingly, prayer becomes more difficult! We discover that the Lord's ways are truly not our ways! Up until now we have been able to explain our dryness in prayer by the unsteadiness of our fidelity, of our commitment. Whenever we were faithful in going to the pump, the water of devotion seemed to flow freely. Now that we have really committed ourselves, it seems clear that there will always be an abundance of water, that the experience of God's presence will be a habitual part of our lives. And for some time that will probably be true, as the Lord strengthens and confirms the commitment we have made. One day, however (sooner or later, depending on our strength and God's designs for us), we go to the pump and find the well dry! We are distressed. Since we discovered the waters of consolation, it has seemed that dryness was almost always traceable to our own lack of fidelity and generosity. We ask anxiously: Where have we failed now? Why is God displeased with us? Why has he again become silent, absent? And if we cannot pinpoint the cause in our behavior, we become even more troubled. We feel like Job; obviously we have offended God in some way, but we cannot discover how. It seems that he is cruel not to show us where we have displeased him.

We said earlier, however, that the Lord never treats us in this way. He never makes us guess how we have offended him. This means that we are now entering a whole new world, where the dryness of the well has an entirely different meaning. Teresa has really given us that meaning in her discussion of the cross. But we might ask: Why the cross? It cannot be simply "the will of God," in the sense that he wants it just because he wants it. We have said that God does not enjoy misery, that he is perfect goodness and love. Thus, if death is the way to life, the cross the path to victory, there must be some reason why this is so—a reason rooted not in the goodness of God but in our own flawed natures.

The cross of desolation is not just a whim of God, it is the only way we can truly learn to love. Even if we are faithful to the Lord, our fidelity is human and thus tainted by sin. Even the just man sins seven times a day. "If we say, 'We have no sin,' we are deceiving ourselves, and truth has no place in us" (1 Jn 1:8). In those who have truly committed themselves to the Lord, there is probably no malice in such failings, but there is still much sickness, much that needs to be healed and forgiven.[7] The instinctual side of us, particularly our vanity and sensuality, remains very much "unredeemed" long after our wills are wholly committed to the Lord of love. This vanity and sensuality need to be burned out of us if ever we are to love as we are loved. This is the reason for the cross: Only by dying to all in ourselves that hinders love can we truly begin to live in love.

• • •

Why Desolating Dryness?

How, then, does the cross of dryness effect this healing? In his classic rules for discernment St. Ignatius Loyola helps to clarify and explain Teresa's insistence on the cross. He says there are three reasons why God may permit desolation.[8] The first is our own negligence, which we have discussed already. But there are two other reasons, closely connected, which Ignatius gives: By desolation "God may try us to test our worth, and the progress we have made in his service and praise"; and "He may wish to give us a true knowledge and understanding . . . that it is not within our power to acquire or retain great devotion, ardent love, tears, or any other spiritual consolation, but that all of this is a gift and grace of God our Lord." Thus, dryness may be permitted by the Lord "to test our worth" or to teach us "that it is not within our power to acquire" genuine consolation, which is purely "a gift and grace of God our Lord."

The latter explanation is clear enough. Strictly speaking, there are no techniques of prayer. The experience of God is sheer grace. It is his free gift, and he gives it when and as he wills. The experience of dryness teaches us this, that we cannot produce God or his consolation ourselves. We can only dispose ourselves for his coming and beseech him to come. In fact, if we never experienced dryness, if we were always able to experience the consolations of God whenever we wished, we might well doubt whether it is really God we are encountering. St. John of the Cross noted this on one occasion, when someone asked him the question: "How do we know it is really God we are encountering and not just our own imagination?" John's reply was this: The best proof that it is really God is that he is often absent when we seek him, and present when we are not seeking him or perhaps don't even want him present. As a reluctant youth entering the seminary, I would have been very happy if the Lord had been absent—or at least not so insistently present. Many times in the years that followed I was very unhappy because he seemed to be absent when I very much wanted him to be present. This frustrating independence of the Lord, says John, is the best proof that he is not just a figment of my imagination. If he were, I could produce him at will. Or I could find a purely natural explanation (like a bad night's sleep) to explain his absence.

Ignatius also says that the Lord may permit desolation to "test our worth and the progress we have made." This clearly could not mean a test in the sense of an examination—since God knows our worth very well, and does not need to give us an exam to find it out! Nor could the purpose of the examination be to teach us our worth, since in that case this reason for desolation would be the same as the one we have discussed in the preceding paragraph. I take "test" here to be used in the sense in which we say that steel is "tested" by fire—that is, it is purified, made strong. All the impurities (air bubbles, foreign matter) are burned out in the fire-testing of steel, and the resulting metal is far stronger than the original iron. Similarly, dryness and desolation purify our love of all the selfishness and vanity which contaminate it, and make our love as strong as steel, "as strong as death" (Sg 8:6). It is in the furnace of dryness that our love is tempered and made divine, so that we can "know just as fully as I am myself known" (1 Cor 13:12), with the knowledge and love of God.

When we see the dryness of prayer in this light, we can appreciate its value. But our question, when we actually experience it, is "How long, O Lord, how long?" As we shall see in Part Two of this book, "From Loving to Truly Loving," the answer is "Very long, indeed!" That would be quite discouraging were it not for the fact that, by the time dryness becomes the normal pattern of our prayer life, we have come to realize what God is doing and to desire that he do it. Then dryness is not desolation, because we are not anxious, fearful, doubting about what the Lord is doing. We have freely submitted ourselves to the fire of his purifying love.

• • •

God's Gentle Pedagogy

Before dryness becomes the normal pattern of our prayer, though, there is usually a lengthy period, after we have really committed ourselves wholeheartedly to the Lord, of alternating consolation and dryness. The well is not continually dry. Sometimes there is abundant water of consolation, and at other times everything is dry. The difficult part of it is that we do not seem able to control or even predict the pattern. No longer can we see a direct link between our own negligence and the dryness of our prayer, and often John's statement about God being absent when we want him and present when we don't expect him seems frustratingly true. When we expect that he will surely be close—as on a great feast or an anniversary which has much personal meaning to us—we are left high and dry. Places and situations which have been blessed by a deep encounter with him in the past now leave us empty, contrary to all our expectations. Then on an ordinary day, in a most unexpected place, he suddenly returns.

What is he doing? As Ignatius says, he is teaching us that he is Lord and not we. He is "testing," purifying our love of all the tendencies we have to seek to control the relationship. The alternating rhythm of consolation and dryness is his way of teaching us to let him be the Lord of the relationship, to give him the complete freedom to come and go in our lives as he wishes. I have noted a similar pattern in my own retreats and in many of the retreats I have directed. At the beginning of the retreat our first effort is to come to quiet before the Lord. Our lives are busy and our minds are filled with many preoccupations as we begin retreat. Our first need is to settle down, to empty our minds of all the noises of our busy lives, to focus our attention on the Lord. Depending on how well rested we are and how well prepared psychologically and spiritually for the retreat, we may come to quiet quickly or it may take us some time— even two or three days—to be really still and attentive. (This is why a retreat of less than eight days can be unsatisfactory for a mature Christian. If the time is shorter than that, we find ourselves just beginning to harvest the fruit when the retreat is finished.) However long it takes, we expect that, once we are quiet, we will surely experience the Lord. But very often we do not . . . at least not right away. He seems to be saying: "I'm glad you have taken the retreat seriously and have come to quiet. But now you must wait for me! I must be the Lord of our encounter, and you cannot turn me on and off, like a water faucet, whenever you wish!" It makes sense because, after all, he is God. But the waiting can be very frustrating, especially when we think how much we have looked forward to this retreat and how little time we really have before it will be over. Teresa tells us not to be disturbed by these thoughts, since God can do in a few moments what would take us years of labor (if indeed we could ever do it): "The time will come when the Lord will repay him all at once. He doesn't fear that the labor is being wasted. He is serving a good Master whose eyes are upon him."[9]

How many times I have experienced this myself! It seemed that all the prayer time was spent in waiting, and I was not very graceful or patient about it. I would perhaps complain to the Lord about it or ask him what in me was preventing his coming. Sometimes the hours of prayer seemed everlasting, and I had great sympathy for Teresa shaking the sand in her sixteenth-century hourglass to make the hour go faster! But when the Lord came, when I experienced his presence at long last, all the waiting seemed short enough, considering the joy of the actual encounter. I knew what Teresa meant in saying "he shall receive his whole reward at once." I felt very sorry for all my impatience and complaining, at least for the moment. When the dryness set in again, I would be just as impatient and querulous as before! So the process continued, the alternation of dryness and consolation, for some years. The times of dryness gradually became longer and the experiences of consolation deeper, though I doubt I noticed this gradual change at the time. I did begin to realize, however, the essential point of it all: The Lord had to become and to be the real leader in my prayer life, and thus in all of my life. As Teresa puts it somewhere,[10] I had to learn to seek the God of consolations and not the consolations of God. It was up to him whether or not there was water in the pump. Mysteriously, and without my realizing it, he was actually changing my attitudes. I was learning to "hang loose, let go, float free," precisely by means of the very dryness of the well which seemed so frustrating to me.

As a director I have learned that my experience was not unique. Others may learn the lesson more quickly and more gracefully than I did, but all of those whom the Lord draws to let go of their own meditations and consolations and discover a deeper, more genuine meaning to prayer must experience the same dryness in which the Lord really becomes the Lord of their lives. It seems, from my experience at least, that there is no other way to learn it, since the self-centeredness of original sin is very deeply rooted in us.

• • •

Do I Really "Lose Tom" in Finding God?

Does this mean that my seminarian friend was right in fearing that "in finding God, I may lose Tom"? I am sure it must appear that way to the outsider who has not experienced the drawing of God, or who has never dared to respond to this drawing. The philosophers Friedrich Nietzsche and Jean Paul Sartre speak for many in every age in saying that submission to God destroys or dehumanizes us . . . that God must "die" in human culture and history in order that we may live. Personally, I don't agree. The only "answer" is the experiences and the lives of those who have really given God a chance. Unfortunately, these are comparatively few (though not as few as we might suspect, as I have learned as a director), even among "religious" people. But Teresa, John, the Little Flower, Ignatius, for example, are certainly not spiritless, cowed, bland personalities. Hannah Hurnard can speak for all of them when she describes her experience of silent prayer with a coworker of equally strong temperament and convictions:

> *Sometimes we were so absorbed in his presence that words would not come at all, and whole hours passed in silence. There is nothing in such times of silent communion of making the mind a blank and waiting for ideas to come as it were*

"out of the blue." But rather communion of this kind demands that every part of the mind and will be actively and joyfully handed over to the Lord for him to use. There is nothing passive about it, but the most active cooperation possible, and though at first one may feel desperately dull and heavy, and the thought of prayer and vital communion almost impossible, the Holy Spirit invariably comes to quicken and empower, so that by the end of those mornings of prayer, we had not only listened to the Lord, and been led to victories of faith, but our minds and bodies had also undergone a wonderful renewal of strength and refreshment.[11]

The perfect example, of course, of this "active and joyful handing over" of oneself to God is the Lord Jesus. He was totally given to the Father, and yet there was nothing passive or timid about him . . . despite some of the frightful, effeminate pictures of him that pass as religious art! He was consumed by a passion for God. He was totally surrendered: "By myself I can do nothing; I can judge only as I am told to judge, and my judging is just, because I seek to do not my own will but the will of him who sent me." He was totally free: "The Father loves me, because I lay down my life in order to take it up again. No one takes it from me; I lay it down of my own free will, and as I have power to lay it down, so I have power to take it up again; and this is the command I have received from my Father" (Jn 5:30; 10:17–18).

In finding God, do I lose Tom? Will the experience of the dry well produce a faceless, timid person? The only "proof" that the answer is "no" is the experience of those, especially the Lord Jesus himself, who have really surrendered to God.

The ultimate proof is to go to the dry well oneself and see what wonders the Lord works.

PART TWO

FROM LOVING
TO TRULY LOVING

4

THE POTTER'S CLAY

• • •

The life of prayer is perhaps the most mysterious dimension of all human experience. We come to be at home with a God we cannot see. We discover that it is only by giving ourselves away totally that we truly come to possess ourselves, that we are most free when most surrendered. We begin to realize that light is darkness and darkness light. We become lost in a trackless desert—and then, if we persevere despite our disorientation, we begin to realize that it is only in being lost, in losing ourselves, that we are found. The whole of our life, and not just our prayer life, becomes a paradox, an apparent contradiction concealing and revealing a deeper truth, because we begin to realize that we must live as we pray. The darkness, giving, surrendering, and lostness cannot be restricted to that one hour a day which we call our "time for prayer." The Lord refuses to be a compartmentalized God; we come to realize that "my work is my prayer," but in an entirely different and much deeper sense than that in which this phrase is usually uttered today.

The work of the prophet is the work of God, because the word the prophet speaks is spoken by God. St. Ignatius

Loyola speaks of his ideal Jesuit as an *"instrumentum con-junctum cum Deo,"* an instrument shaped to the hand of God, a "perfect fit." But this is true not only of the ideal Jesuit, or even the ideal priest or religious, but of the ideal Christian—including the Christian whose call is to raise a family to the glory of God. It is as true of my brother and sister-in-law, whose primary vocation now is to raise six children, as it is of me. Those children are every bit as much the concern of God—the primary responsibility of God—as are all the people he sends to me in my priestly ministry.

When my brother and sister-in-law read this, they may well think: "That's all very nice in theory, and deep down we believe it, but in practice it is impossible to live. It's all well and good for the sisters and priests, who have plenty of time to get to know God and to submit to his mysterious ways; but we have trouble enough just surviving the crises of each day and getting to bed exhausted each night." Unbeknownst to my brother and sister-in-law, the busy priests and sisters who read this will probably say much the same thing: "The stress on prayer is beautiful in theory, and in the seminary or novitiate I saw something of what it could mean, but it is not realistic to pursue it in the hectic life of the parish. That kind of life, at least in this world, is only for contemplatives." What the poor contemplatives can say I don't know! Everyone drawn to prayer feels that "contemplatives" are the spoiled children of the Lord, who have every opportunity to experience fully all Teresa's four ways of drawing water. Yet, in my experience as a director of contemplatives, the percentage who really reach the heart of God is probably not much greater than among married people and active religious. They, poor souls, can only blame it on the community life or the work by which they support themselves. The excuses of the married are no longer available to them.

I mention this here not to justify the value or importance of prayer; I presume that anyone who has read this far in a book like this one is convinced of that. Rather, my point is that all these excuses miss the mark. The real problem of the interior life is not that we don't have the time or the proper conditions to live it. Even the hermit living in total isolation in his rocky cave will always find bats and snakes and mosquitoes to explain why his prayer life has stagnated. The snakes and the parish meetings and the children are real enough; I do not intend to deny that. But the hard fact remains that some people in each of these lives, confronted with each of these obstacles, do come to a genuine and deep life with God. None of these obstacles by itself makes a solid prayer life impossible.

• • •

The Real Problem

What really hinders our growth is that we don't really want badly enough to discover God in our lives. We do want it in some sense or else we would not have come this far. But the mystery, the paradox, the incongruity of God's ways, the "cost of discipleship" . . . all give us pause. It is much easier to say "circumstances prevent me from going on" than to say "the cost is too great." That is why I have always loved the rich young man of Luke 18; he went away sad, but he was honest. He made no excuses, no rationalizations. I have often thought that eventually his honesty must have been blessed by the courage to return and follow the Lord wholeheartedly.

What is this "cost" which makes so many fall by the wayside in the life of prayer? It might appear at first that it is the demand of responding adequately to the love of an all-holy, all-perfect God. Good people have told me they found themselves filled with both joy and apprehension when confronted with the love of God. The joy of his presence was very real, but the apprehension came because they knew themselves, their selfishness and frailty, well enough to doubt that they could really live worthy of such a love. I believe this apprehension is mistaken; we are not called to respond adequately to the love of God, because none of us can ever do so. It is simply impossible for us to love as we are loved by God.

From what we have seen in Part One of this book, we can affirm that the call of God is not so much to do something as to allow something to be done in us. This was the whole point of Teresa's metaphor of the four ways of drawing water. As we grow, we do less and less and God does more and more until, when the rains come, he is doing everything. The problem and the challenge which confront the one who prays are ultimately not to do but to surrender. This is really what blocks our growth: not the active demands of responding to God but the cost of giving up our self-determination. The snakes and parish meetings are simply excuses to avoid the demand of letting go of our lives.

It is true, of course, that we do something, particularly at the beginning of our prayer life. Part Two of *Opening to God* is filled with "things to do": techniques for coming to quiet, actively purifying the soul, meditating and contemplating. That is, in fact, probably why so many get stuck at step one of their interior lives. They find satisfaction in all the doing it entails and are unwilling to imagine a prayer life which is not busy with thoughts and resolutions, insights and affections and applications to their daily activities. All this is good in itself, of course, and should be the pattern of our prayer as long as it is fruitful for us. But, if human experience and the great writers on prayer are to be believed, this pattern will not usually last forever. While it lasts, *Opening to God* or a similar book is the only guide necessary. Yet many people have written to me since *Opening to*

God appeared and asked: "When is the sequel coming? You left me hanging! When I read the epilogue I began to find myself, but you were finished!" *When the Well Runs Dry* is written for them—and, thank God, they are many. But, as I hope Part One has already made clear, the answer to their question, "What do I do next?" is "You do less and less and God does more and more." This is the letting go, hanging loose, floating free of which I spoke earlier. It begins when we begin to draw water with a pump, and our own exertion becomes a much less significant part of the whole activity.

As our prayer moves "from knowing to loving" (as Part One is entitled), from the head to the heart, the activity of our understanding and imagination tends to be less important, and these faculties are reduced to a secondary role, which I described as "remembering." Many people are able to accept this "inactivity" of their intellects; many others, perhaps especially the more intelligent, are not, and their growth is blocked. Our wills and feelings must now carry the principal burden of our labor in prayer. The heart becomes central and very active.

When the water of devotion stops flowing, the feelings also dry up and the will seems paralyzed. This is the time the well runs dry, since the water of which Teresa speaks is devotion or consolation. As we said in chapter 3, this usually happens only occasionally and for more or less brief periods at this stage of our prayer life. What the Lord is teaching us is that he must be the Lord of the encounter, that it is up to him to determine the rainy seasons and the dry seasons of the spirit. At this point we experience, at least for certain periods, the inactivity of our feelings. Again, the challenge is to accept this dryness and to surrender our control over our own feelings. I suspect that many people, especially today when there is so much stress on the felt experience of God, find their interior growth impeded here. We go to a prayer meeting, a liturgy, a session alone in the chapel, expecting to feel something. If we do not have a religious experience we feel cheated and our fervor for prayer cools off. We tend to identify prayer with feeling something.

• • •

Periodic Dryness and the Potter's Clay

Even those who have some depth to their relationship with the Lord will describe to me their dry times as unfruitful—as so much dead space between the moments of real encounter. They are quite surprised when I suggest to them that probably their dry hours were their best prayer. How can that be, when these hours seem so fruitless? The reason is because at these times our prayer is likely to be most unselfish, most "God-centered," provided we persevere despite the dryness. We are learning, as Teresa puts it, "to seek the God of consolations and not the consolations of God."

As long as there is an alternation of consolation and desolation, periods of devotion and periods of dryness, we can learn to survive the dryness for the sake of the times when God is close. It is difficult, but we learn that God is teaching us to let him be the Lord of the encounter, as we saw in chapter 3. Then we can accept the dryness and even see its value in purifying our love. The most beautiful biblical image of this experience is the story of the potter and his clay in Jeremiah 18:1–6. When those I am directing reach this point of periodic dryness, not only of the understanding but also of the feelings, I often suggest that they spend some days or weeks praying over this brief passage. Many have found it extremely fruitful, and it has become, in fact, the guiding image for their prayer life thereafter. Jeremiah tells us:

> The word that came to Jeremiah from Yahweh is
> as follows, "Get up and make your way down to

*the potter's house, and there I shall tell you what
I have to say." So I went down to the potter's
house; and there he was, working at the wheel.
But the vessel he was making came out wrong, as
may happen with clay when a potter is at work.
So he began again and shaped it into another vessel, as he thought fit. Then the word of Yahweh
came to me as follows, "House of Israel, can I not
do to you what this potter does?" Yahweh speaks.
"Yes, like clay in the potter's hand, so you are in
mine, House of Israel."*

In its original setting, the story of the potter is an allegory for the way Yahweh is dealing with his unfaithful people,
Israel. It was written about 600 BC, when Israel had a weak
king, Jehoiachin, and had fallen under foreign domination.
Within a few years the monarchy begun 400 years earlier
by Saul and David would cease to exist. Israel was no longer an independent nation. The Babylonian Captivity was
about to begin, perhaps the greatest national tragedy in the
whole history of Israel. In these circumstances, the meaning
of Yahweh's word to Jeremiah is clear: Israel is the clay in
the hands of Yahweh, the potter; she has turned out badly
in his hand, and now she is to be broken and refashioned
according to the potter's designs for her.

However, each of us, just as much as Israel, is the clay
in the potter's hands. This is why the story still speaks so
beautifully to us today. The Lord is the potter; he is the one
who designs the pot in his mind; he is the one who shapes
the clay according to his plan. The clay cannot shape itself;
it does not even know what is to be made of it. A vase? A
pitcher? A candlestick? Only the potter knows! The image
does not sit very well with educated people today, who feel
that such a God is a threat to our full humanity. We are much
more comfortable with the idea that the will of God for us is

that we take responsibility for the consequences of our own choices. The image of the potter seems to dehumanize us, to destroy our personal freedom and responsibility, to keep us forever childlike. There is a genuine intellectual, speculative problem here—one which we have already confronted more than once.[1] At this point, however, I merely wish to stress that, whether we understand God's ways or not, the image of the potter and the clay perfectly expresses the reason for the dryness of the well. The Lord is the potter and we are the clay; the Lord is the source of the living waters we long to drink. We must learn to let him be Lord.

• • •

Prolonged Dryness: Breaking and Refashioning the Clay

This much we have already explained in the preceding chapter. But it is not the final lesson of the interior life, and I have introduced Jeremiah's image of the clay now because I think it can also give us light and guidance for the next stage of the journey. The picture Yahweh presents through Jeremiah is brief and simple, and yet I find it extraordinarily rich. Once we have learned, by God's grace, to accept the fact that he is the potter and we the clay, that consolation and devotion, if they are genuine, are purely his gift, what happens to our prayer life? It would be nice to be able to say that we have reached our goal and are ready to possess or be possessed by God fully. But the truth of the matter is that we are really just beginning! We are ready to begin to know the Lord, as St. John of the Cross says.

What happens now is that we start to discover that the dryness of our prayer life is not merely to teach us to let go, to allow the Lord to be the boss. It is, rather, by means of this very dryness that he accomplishes the major part of the work of transformation which is really what our prayer life is all about. In order to love God truly we must, as incredible as it seems to say it, be made divine. True love can only exist between equals, and thus we can only "know as we are known," love as we are loved, when we have been divinized. This is why Jesus can tell the disciples: "You must be made perfect as your heavenly Father is perfect" (Mt 5:48). But, as we noted earlier, the key words here are "be made." We cannot do it ourselves. If we are to be divine, to be made perfect as the Father is perfect, it can only be because God dwells in us and works our transformation.

Thus we can see that the Lord is not merely teaching us that he is boss in order to assert his authority, his lordship. He is not status-conscious and anxious that we grovel before him as before some absolutist monarch. If that were true we would still be servants and the whole purpose of our prayer life would be to affirm and reinforce our servitude. There are great religions in which this vision of God and humanity prevails, but Christianity is not one of them. Rather, the reason for our loving surrender to God is that we desire to be able to love as we are loved, and only the Lord can effect in us the transformation which this demands. The clay cannot shape itself, cannot even have an idea of what it would mean to become a vase or a candlestick or an "Adam" into whom life can be breathed. Only the potter can envision what the clay might be, and only his skilled hands can realize his vision. And we are the clay in the hands of the divine potter, to be fashioned into a living and life-giving Spirit after the model of Jesus our Brother (see 1 Cor 15:45).

This theme of our transformation, our divinization, is a central preoccupation of Paul, especially in Romans 8 and 1 Corinthians 15. It is God's great work in us, so deep and mysterious that Paul ends one description of it with an exclamation of praise "to him whose power, working in us, can do infinitely more than we can ask or imagine" (Eph 3:20). And John speaks of the same mystery of our transformation in these beautiful words: "My dear friends, we are already God's children, but what we shall be in the future has not yet been revealed. We are well aware that when it appears, we shall be like him, because we shall see him as he really is" (1 Jn 3:2). This is the reason why we lose control—not because God desires that we grovel before him, but because the tremendous new thing which is taking place in us can only be his work.

As our prayer life matures, we become more and more aware of being the clay in the hands of the potter. The clay can do virtually nothing to transform itself into an object of beauty. But it can be soft, pliable, sensitive to the potter's touch. People often talk about their fear that God's will may break them, that what he asks is too hard for them to bear. And yet the clay is never broken by anything the potter may do to it—unless the clay has become hard and rigid. As long as it is malleable it will never break, but once it begins to resist the potter's touch, to push against his shaping, it will be very much in danger of breaking. This is what happened to Israel, and that is why Yahweh sent Jeremiah to tell her that she needed to be broken in order to be refashioned according to the potter's design. Even her breaking was not to be for her destruction, but for her healing.

So it is with us. By sin we are misshapen. The image of God in us has been deformed, and the disfigurement has hardened in the clay. As long as we are content with our shape, the attempts of the potter to refashion us and to transform our ugliness will seem very threatening and frightening to us. Recall what we said earlier about knowledge of God and knowledge of self going hand in hand. But, as we begin to realize what we really are and what we might be, the breaking which is necessary for transformation, while still painful, is no longer threatening. As we grow a bit more we even come to desire this breaking because of the longing to become like him which the Lord of love has implanted deeply in us. We want the cross because we have glimpsed the glory to which it leads. We can understand what made Paul say: "I want to be gone and to be with Christ, and this is by far the stronger desire" (Ph 1:23).

• • •

Surgery and Anesthesia: John's Night of the Sense

We do not come to that depth of desire overnight, of course. It is, in fact, the fruit of many years of purifying prayer in the lives of those who pray faithfully. It is the deeper reason for the dryness which gradually becomes the usual pattern of our prayer and not just an occasional experience in a generally consoling prayer life. Like a patient who has been anesthetized in order that lifesaving surgery may be performed, the one who prays now finds himself or herself experiencing a dryness, a darkness, a paralysis of the mind and the feelings which is the anesthesia of the interior life. Since we usually do not understand what is happening at such a time, the experience is very frustrating. Moreover, it is rare that we can find a guide who really understands what is happening to us. We feel that we have somehow lost God, precisely when we have learned to desire him greatly. It is an agonizing experience, truly a dark night which seems to have no ending.

Adults who understand the necessity and value of radical surgery can still find it a fearsome prospect when they have to face it. How much more frightening it must be to a child who does not understand why the pain is necessary to save his life! He fears, in fact, that the "bad man" only wants to hurt him, and he cannot understand why his parents have betrayed him by handing him over to suffering. How hard it is to explain to the child that we allow him to suffer the pain precisely because we love him. The hardest thing for the parents is not the physical suffering of the child, which after all is the road to health and healing, but rather the uncomprehending fear which grips him. If only the child can be brought to see, in some small way, that the pain is really for his good, that we allow it because we love him. When he begins to comprehend this and to accept it, he becomes courageous and peaceful, and so do we.

When it comes to the surgery which the Lord must perform on us to transform and divinize us, we are all uncomprehending children at first. The ways of God and the health to which he seeks to bring us are totally beyond our natural imagining. Yet, all of us are "sick unto death" in the life of the Spirit, so much so that most of us never seem to suspect the better life to which we are called. Once we begin to take seriously the life of prayer, we are already on the road to this better life. That means, inevitably, that the "radical surgery" of the Spirit awaits us. When the time of this radical surgery of prolonged dryness comes, we are like terrified children who take for disaster what is really salvation. This is perhaps the most crucial moment on the whole journey to God. St. John of the Cross calls it the "night of sense" and says that it is "common and happens to many" who give themselves seriously to a life of prayer.[2]

Yet, John says, not many successfully traverse this night to emerge into the divine light of a new day. It is not that God's grace is lacking, but rather that our generosity, our courage, our openness to God are limited. This limits what the grace of God can do in us. As we have stressed before, he never forces himself upon us or works in us beyond what we are willing to allow him to do. If we do not grow in love, it is not because his love for us is limited, but because we set limits to what his love can do in us.

This is an important point. Too often we assume that growth in prayer is only for holy people, and that the holy are somehow those who have been favored by God more than most men and women. Thus, in reading the preceding paragraphs we can easily say: "But that is too difficult for me! I am just an ordinary person, not a saint. That kind of purification leading to that kind of love is beyond me!" But notice that what we have been saying has a close analogy in the way married couples are called to love each other. In the marriage ceremony, they give themselves to each other "for better or worse." I have been privileged to celebrate the marriages of several of my former students. Each time I ask them to repeat that phrase after me, I wonder if they truly realize what they are promising. I doubt that they do. When we are young and romantic, we say "for better or worse" and we are sincere, but what we mean is, I hope and believe it will all be "better," but if the "worse" comes I will try to survive it with God's grace. It never enters our minds that the "worse" is just as necessary to the growth of love as is the "better." Yet, that is true. The hard times are not obstacles to the growth of love, although they will certainly seem to be such when we are young. Rather, they are a necessary part of the experience by which real love comes to be.

I myself learned this lesson most strikingly at the time when my father was dying. I was called home to his deathbed three and a half weeks before he died. During those weeks I sat with my mother in the hospital room and saw him die day by day. But the most striking thing was that I saw her die day by day with him. Their lives had been one for forty-two years, so much so that she lived his experience of dying with him. I gradually came to realize that this experience was an essential part of the whole history of their love for each other. It was certainly the "worse" to which my mother had vowed herself forty-two years before, and it did something to the quality of their love which could never have been accomplished by all the "better" times of those long years together. In a bittersweet way, it was a beautiful experience for me, one whose value was very clear. In fact, I think it was then that I came to appreciate much of what the Lord was doing in my life. I realized that any love, whether it be for God or for people, comes to maturity in the hard times. It is the living through these hard times together that gives the good times their real depth and richness, as we realize the meaning of a genuinely selfless love which perdures through, and finds expression in, all the shifting moods and circumstances of our life together.

Thus a really good marriage is just as costly as a genuine interior life with God. It is probably almost as rare, too, and for the same reasons. This is why Gabriel Marcel, Rosemary Haughton, and others have seen real human love as the essential road to God for most people. We learn in flesh-and-blood circumstances the real meaning of love; we also discover that even the deepest human love leaves us some-how incomplete unless it is rooted in God, who can ground a love which is total self-giving and survives beyond death. The need is in every man and woman; these pages are writ-ten for those men and women, few or many as they may be, who have come to experience that need in themselves.

● ● ●

"This Night Is Contemplation"

The peculiar problem in prayer is that we cannot see God as we see a spouse or a friend. Even if we have become convinced of our need for him and of the transforming value of the hard times (in our life of prayer, the dryness), how do we "read the face of God"? How do we know what he is doing in our lives, or even that the dryness is really his doing? This is where direction and the guidance of the mas-ters of prayer become crucial to our growth. Fortunately, one of the greatest of these masters has left us clear and suc-cinct guidelines for our life in the interior desert. St. John of the Cross has set down in two or three brief chapters the classic description of this desert experience (which he calls the "dark night") and the authoritative guidelines as to how we should act. For me, John's short discussion is one of the most important passages in the whole literature of prayer.[3] He first explains what is really happening in this dark night (chapter VIII); then he gives three signs by which we can recognize that our dryness really is the dark night and not due to some natural cause (chapter IX); finally, he tells us how we should act in the face of this experience (chapter X). Since I have seen so many people helped by what John has to say, I should like to explain and comment on each of these points.

To begin, let us recall the situation of the person at this stage of the spiritual life. Her prayer has moved from the head to the heart, from knowing to loving; then, after a honeymoon period when the waters of devotion flowed freely, she has experienced a lengthy period of alternating consolation and dryness, where the Lord was teaching her that consolation is a free gift of God, not to be achieved by our own efforts according to our own timetable. Now that she has learned to let go and to let the Lord be the boss, she finds herself experiencing an almost continuous dryness. God seems to be totally absent, despite a great desire to encounter him. It is as if God has seduced her only to turn away at the last moment. Even if her head believes all we have said about the value to true love of hard times, her heart is miserable since she cannot read the face of God to discern whether this is really the hard times which deepen love, or rather a case of total abandonment by a God whose holiness is forever beyond her.

John's first word is his deepest. He says, at the beginning of chapter VIII, that "this night . . . is contemplation."[4] The darkness is not because God is so far away, but because he is so close. The image I have often used is the following: If you are praying in a dark chapel at night, with only the vigil light burning, and someone enters and suddenly turns on the lights, you are momentarily blinded. Your eyes had grown accustomed to the dark. Now you cannot see, not because there is too little light, but because there is too much.

Similarly, our spiritual eyes are accustomed to the darkness of earthly things. We are like bats which can only see in the dark and are blinded by the light. Even our prayer life has been "in the dark," by means of thoughts and images and feelings appropriate to knowing the things of this world. We have felt that we came to know God by means of these thoughts and images, but in reality it is impossible for the infinite God to be captured by our finite thoughts, images, and feelings. Now, when everything suddenly becomes dark, when our ordinary ways of knowing are blinded, it is because the light of God has suddenly been turned on in us and our eyes cannot stand the light. This is what John means by contemplation: an immediate experience of God as he is in himself, as contrasted with a mediate, indirect experience through our own thoughts and feelings. This experience is thoughtless, and even wordless, because all our activities inevitably distort and render indirect the reality of God in himself.

Since we cannot imagine and never even suspected there was any other way of knowing and loving except through our own thoughts, this is a profoundly disturbing and disorienting experience. Just as the child, who is being weaned from milk so that he will learn to eat solid food, may be confused since he cannot imagine any other food besides milk, so we, too, fear that everything is lost. We truly desire to know and love God in himself, to be able to reach out and touch him; but when he comes very close to us we are blinded and feel we have lost even the contact with him that we had before. Just the opposite is really true: God is closer than ever! Here we begin to discover a reason for the dryness and the darkness we experience—a reason deeper than our learning to let God be the boss. We said in chapter 3 that the alternation of consolation and dryness teaches us to let go, hang loose, float free, and to allow the good God truly to be the Lord of the encounter we seek. Now, as the dryness and darkness become more a constant pattern of our prayer, we discover that it is much more than God's way of asserting his sovereignty. The darkness is actually "contemplation," a whole new way of praying in which we truly become the clay in the hands of the potter. It is dark because it is totally beyond our natural capacities. Yet it is precisely in this dark prayer that we are transformed, made divine. Our hearts are stretched so that they may be able to hold the infinite God; our eyes are purified so that they may be able to see the blinding light that is our God.

St. Augustine expresses beautifully what is really happening in the darkness, when he is commenting on the words of the first epistle of St. John: "We shall be like him, for we shall see him as he really is" (1 Jn 3:2). Augustine says:

> *The entire life of a good Christian is an exercise in holy desire. You do not see what you long for, but the very act of desiring prepares you, so that when he comes you may see and be utterly satisfied. Suppose you are going to fill some holder or container, and you know you will be given a large amount. Then you set about stretching your sack or wineskin or whatever it is. Why? Because you know the quantity you will have to put in it, and your eyes tell you there is not enough room. By stretching it, therefore, you increase the capacity of the sack, and this is how God deals with us. Simply by making us wait he increases our desire, which in turn enlarges the capacity of our soul, making it able to receive what is to be given to us.*[5]

125

God is stretching our finite hearts by means of his direct, dark presence to our souls. For us it seems to be just "waiting," and a painful waiting at that, because we are being stretched by hands we cannot see with our natural faculties.

• • •

John of the Cross's
Three Signs of the Dark Night

In chapter 5, we shall have to try to explain more fully this experience of dark waiting. First, let us consider the signs John of the Cross gives us "for discerning whether the dryness is the result of this purgation."[6] The problem is that the aridity or darkness could be due to our own sinfulness or negligence, or it could be due to "some bad humor or indisposition of the body." All of us have experienced times of sickness, when we thought we would have plenty of time to pray and yet found ourselves totally lethargic and unable even to think about the Lord. How can we tell whether the prolonged dryness we experience is due to our own sickness or sinfulness, or whether it is really God working in us by means of this dark contemplation? John gives three signs which I have found extremely helpful, both in my own life and in my work as a director.

The first sign is that while "a soul finds no pleasure or consolation in the things of God, it also fails to find it in anything created." My prayer seems empty and dry and even distasteful, but when I try to escape the frustration by busying myself with other things—external occupations, frivolities—they leave me equally empty and dissatisfied. I recall a very prayerful sister telling me of her experience: God seemed so far away and so uninterested in her that she finally said to him: "All right! If you don't care, then neither do I!" And she tried to avoid prayer and go her own way, even to "sin"! But she was equally miserable away from prayer! This sounds like a bad situation, and yet John says her experience makes it very likely that the misery, the dryness, is not due to her "recently committed sins or imperfections."

If this desolation were due to her own negligence, then she would feel "some inclination to taste other things than those of God; since, whenever the desire is allowed indulgence in any imperfection, it immediately feels inclined thereto." That is, if the dryness of prayer is due to my own culpable infidelity, I will find myself drawn to "low and earthly things" (St. Ignatius' phrase), and will gradually seek my satisfaction more and more in them to the neglect of prayer. This often happens to relative beginners among the seminarians who make a fervent retreat but then gradually drift back to the sensual gratifications of daily life and thus neglect prayer more and more. My sister-friend, however, was unable to drift: she was just as miserable running away from the Lord as she was seeking him. How surprised (even unbelieving, at first) she was when I told her that her experience was probably a sign something good and deep was happening!

John says, though, that this sign alone is not sufficient to be sure that our dryness is due to God's dark presence in contemplation. This "lack of enjoyment in things above or below might (also) proceed from some indisposition of melancholy humor (sickness), which oftentimes makes it impossible for the soul to take pleasure in anything." Hence he suggests a second sign which should also characterize the authentic dark night: "The memory is ordinarily centered upon God, with painful care and solicitude, thinking that it is not serving God, but is backsliding, because it finds itself without sweetness in the things of God." The key phrase here is "with painful care and solicitude." God seems far away and I seem unworthy of his love, but I am drawn to him nonetheless, like a magnet. I am miserable with him and even more miserable without him. (How well I remember the years when that sentence summarized for me the greater part of my prayer experience!) I can't find him and yet I desperately need to find him. Why would John call this wretched state a good sign? Can we really be drawing closer to our goal precisely when it seems everything is lost? John says that if the dark dryness is due to sickness (or to our own negligence) we will not experience this "painful care and solicitude" to find the Lord. If we are negligent we will not feel solicitous to find him, but eager to escape his threatening presence. And if we are sick we won't feel anything at all. Our desire for God will be, as it were, anesthetized. Thus our very pain and solicitude are a sign, contrary to everything we would naturally think, that the God we seek is truly at work in us drawing us to himself.

At this point, John begins to explain what it is that God is doing in us. For the sake of clarity, however, let us save this explanation for the following chapter and turn instead to the third sign he gives that our experience is genuine dark contemplation. He says that the third sign is "the powerlessness, in spite of one's efforts, to meditate and make use of the imagination, the interior sense, as was one's previous custom. At this time God does not communicate Himself through the senses as He did before, by means of discursive analysis and synthesis of ideas, but begins to communicate Himself through pure spirit, by an act of simple contemplation, in which there is no discursive succession of thought."[7] We have seen something of what this means above, when we spoke of the fact that our finite faculties cannot grasp the infinite God. And we noted in chapter 3 that this inability to meditate or contemplate imaginatively begins when we begin to draw water by means of the pump. At that time, however, our faculties still do assist the will by what we called "remembering," at least at times. Their blankness is only more or less occasional and transient. Here, however, John is speaking of a situation where the soul's "inability to reflect with the faculties grows ever greater . . . and brings the workings of sense to an end."[8] Now our understanding and imagination seem simply useless to our prayer, whether for knowing or for remembering.

I have found this third sign particularly helpful when pray-ers, experiencing the dark night, feel they should "begin all over again"—return to the meditation they gave up long ago. In such a situation, it does not prove helpful just to tell them to trust my judgment. Rather, I find it best to tell them: "Go ahead and try to meditate. If it proves fruitful then perhaps you have been too passive and unprepared. But if it is not fruitful to meditate again, then you know your dryness is not due to your own negligence. So you can then abandon your efforts and just be at peace with God's dryness."

Our intellectual faculties are empty; our will seems painfully unable to find its joy in God—and John says these are the sure signs that God is working something truly wonderful in us! If the three signs we have described characterize our prayer, John says we can feel confident that our experience is a genuine dark night of prayer whereby God is effecting a divine transformation in us. What a strange world we have entered, where loss is gain and darkness is light and all our human values seem turned upside down! To one who has never experienced it, it must be nearly incomprehensible. Yet, to those who have experienced the purifying darkness, John's signs will touch some deep point in their being. In fact, I would venture to add this as a fourth sign to the three John gives: When I, as a director, have had occasion to explain John's signs to many troubled persons who were experiencing just what John describes, their reaction was always almost the same: "If I really can believe it is God working, I don't mind the darkness so much. I can live with it and accept it. What really disturbs me is the fear that I have somehow lost God whom I love so much." What really disturbs them is the fear they have lost the Lord. That reaction, which echoes John's second sign, is for me the capstone of all of the signs, the proof that it is indeed God's dark contemplation which they are experiencing. I would then feel sure they can proceed in peace, confident that it is truly the Lord working in them.

• • •

What Then Should We Do?

But if this is so, what should we do? What is our part in a prayer that seems so totally beyond our comprehension? First of all, we should have a good director whose judgment we will trust if he or she says our prayer is authentic, despite the way it appears to us. We should hear God in our director, and not worry about seeking further proof for ourselves. We go to the director precisely to hear God, and we believe it is a sacramental situation. We also believe that the Lord loves us and cares for us more than we care for ourselves. Hence it is up to him to clarify things for us if we are on the wrong track; we should simply proceed in peace on the word of the director and leave everything else to the Lord.[9]

As regards our prayer itself, John says that we should simply forget about any attempt to reason or meditate when we come to prayer, "since this is not the time for it, but . . . allow the soul to remain in peace and quietness, although it may seem clear to them that they are doing nothing and are wasting their time. . . . The truth is that they will be doing quite sufficient if they have patience and persevere in prayer without making any effort . . . contenting themselves with merely a peaceful and loving attentiveness toward God, and in being without anxiety." We should even be contented "simply with a loving and peaceful attentiveness to God, and live without the concern, without the effort, and without the desire to taste or feel Him. All the desires disquiet the soul and distract it from the peaceful quiet and sweet idleness of contemplation which is being communicated to it."[10]

What a strange state we have come to! We spent the early years of our interior life learning to know God and then to desire him (the move from the head to the heart). Now that this desire to experience him has become the very center of our lives and it is he alone whom we truly desire, John tells us we must be "without desire to have experience of him or to perceive him"! Like Magdalene we had to learn to love him above everything else before he could teach us not to cling to him. Like a young couple courting, our love had to be nurtured and strengthened by frequent presence before we could begin to discover that love is deeper than presence, and can be equally strong in absence.

This absence, as we have seen, is not merely capricious or cruel on the part of the good Lord. We need him to be absent to our natural ways of knowing and loving so that we can give them up for a better way—the divine way. We must learn to "do nothing gracefully" so that the Lord, our Love, will be free to stretch our hearts and our minds to embrace infinity. If we can believe that this is really what is happening, then we can be graceful, "without anxiety," as John says. We can learn to be at home in the dark because we are sure, in faith, that the potter is truly shaping the clay, even though the clay sees nothing of what is happening. Then our dryness is no longer desolation because we are not anxious, fearful, troubled by the dark. In fact, we come to love the dark because we realize that the Light is very close and that our experience of darkness is the only sure way to the eternal vision we so greatly desire.[11] Nor would we rush the potter, since we begin to realize that the vessel he is shaping is intended to last for eternity. In fact, we find the need to pray more, not to experience his presence now, but to give him all the time we can to shape the vessel into which he will delight to pour his love.

5

DARKNESS ABOVE AND
CLOUDS BELOW

• • •

The experience of darkness or dryness, then, becomes more and more the normal, constant pattern of our prayer. John of the Cross tells us that this is not a sign of failure or regression; contrary to our natural ways of judging things, it is a good and healthy sign of real interior growth. In some profoundly mysterious way, the flowers in the garden of the Lord bloom best in times of drought.

The question that inevitably comes to our minds, and troubles our hearts, is: How long will this dry darkness last? We gradually come to accept it as necessary to growth, but we want it to be over with as quickly as possible. We can accept it, but we can't enjoy it—and in our misery we are just hanging on until the Lord returns. When I explain to people whom I direct the meaning of their experience, the inevitable question is: "Yes, but how long will this misery last?" When I say to them, only half-jokingly, "That all depends on how much longer you expect to live!" the response is always a groan and an "Oh, no!" Even those who can see the value of the dryness in purifying their love want to get the purification over with as quickly as possible and get on with the business of loving the Lord. It seems only reasonable to feel this way. After all, the mature person can see and accept the necessity of surgery at certain critical points in life, but no one wants to spend the rest of one's life on the operating table. What would be the value of permanent and perpetual surgery, where we never returned to renewed health and fruitful living?

Such a life, lived perpetually on the operating table, would make no sense. If we knew that to be our fate, it would be wiser to relax and let death come rather than to prolong the agony. But our analogy to surgery also suggests the answer to the dilemma: As long as we seek the fulfillment of our interior lives within the span of our lives on earth, such prolonged dryness will scarcely make sense. Once we realize, however, that our life of prayer is really only the beginning of eternal life, and that the transformation God is working in us is truly the foundation of an eternity of loving him, we begin to see the dryness from quite a different perspective. Death is not the end but the beginning of our life with God. After the first million years in heaven we will still be just beginning to know and love the Lord. Once this realization (so very different from our natural way of viewing time and history) begins to dawn on us, everything seems different. Even if the transforming purification the Lord is working in us should take all of fifty years, those fifty years do not seem so long at all from the perspective of an eternity of loving and being loved.

• • •

The Dry Darkness Is Purgatory

There is another realization which gradually dawns on us and places the dark night in an entirely new light: This dry darkness is really purgatory. I remember when that insight first struck me at prayer; it seemed to be the Lord's word, and yet I wondered if it could really be true. I had always been puzzled by the doctrine of purgatory, particularly by all the talk about fire and smoke and pain. It seemed like a peculiarly vengeful way for an all-good God to act. When the parents of a murder victim demanded the death of the murderer as revenge for their loss, it seemed like a natural human reaction to me, but scarcely Christian. How then could God be demanding vengeance for our sins when his name is Love? But when I began to realize that purgatory is not vengeance but purification and transformation, the whole doctrine seemed not only acceptable but necessary. Sooner or later we have to be made divine if we are going to love as we are loved, if not in this life, then certainly after death. Since most people choose to avoid the call to purifying transformation during this life, it seemed only logical that this call would have to be faced later, since not sooner. The only alternative would be to remain untransformed forever, and that is hell!

What, then, if some souls, drawn by grace, should choose to begin to live eternity now? It seemed to follow that this would first mean living purgatory now, since we can only know and love God as he is (which is eternal life—Jn 17:3) once we have become like him. Becoming like him means, as the gospels make abundantly clear, dying to all in ourselves which is selfishness and sin. This process of purifying transformation (this purgatory) is the central message of the first epistle of John, one of my favorite writings in the New Testament. "God is light; and there is no darkness in him" (1 Jn 1:5); we are darkness and sin (1:8, 10) and Jesus Christ alone, encountered in the community of fraternal love, is our healing; if we live this life in Christ fully, we shall be healed and transformed, until eventually "we shall be like him, because we shall see him as he really is" (3:2).

When I discovered that St. John of the Cross, the great master of prayer, affirms clearly and repeatedly that this dark night is indeed purgatory for some, I was happy and not surprised.[1] It seemed to make sense of an experience which would otherwise be inexplicable, given the goodness of God. Now I could desire that the Lord continue this dark work in me, even though I still didn't enjoy it (since I am no masochist!). I could truly desire it, since I could see that it was the only way to the goal I so greatly desired.

Even before the analogy of purgatory came to my mind, I had a vague realization of what was happening. I can, in fact, recall the very moment when it first struck me. For some years, prayer had been dark and God seemed far away. It seemed I spent most of my time complaining and crying out for relief. Then, one day, during a retreat I was making at the Carmelite convent in Naga City here in the Philippines, the Lord suddenly returned. I was in the third or fourth day of my retreat, and more or less resigned, though unhappily, to the darkness. When the light suddenly reappeared, it was an overwhelming experience. It was morning—I remember well, because when noontime came and I went to lunch, I was walking on the clouds. Yet, as I ate, I just as suddenly realized that I was much more secure in the dark! For years I had complained about it and begged the Lord to show his face to me . . . and only when he did so did I realize the value of the darkness. It is hard to explain just what I realized, but I think it was that I could so easily spoil the light, the consolation of his coming, by my own selfishness and vanity. The dark was a much more secure situation for me, because in that dark prayer there was nothing to gratify my self-seeking and to deflect me from centering wholly on the Lord rather than on myself. I was more secure in the dark—more secure from myself and all in me that could spoil love.

Darkness Is Really Excessive Light

It was a tremendous realization. As always happens at such times, though, I was not sure if the insight was genuine and truly from the Lord. Only time and experience could tell for sure whether it was really he teaching me. When I returned to prayer that afternoon I felt a little foolish. It appeared that all along I had been complaining about what was really a gift, a grace. Not that I saw the darkness as a permanent and perpetual state; after all, the whole purpose of prayer is to know, to possess and be possessed by God. But it seemed that the darkness was the right way for me to travel to the light. Only darkness, for the time being, could burn out everything in me that clouded the light and spoiled love. As I look back over the years, that day still stands as one of the real turning points in my prayer life. Everything that has happened since, in my own life and in the lives of those I direct, has served to confirm the authenticity of the realization I had then. That was the day when I began to be at home in the dark, and the darkness of prayer has had a positive and ever deeper meaning for me since.

St. John of the Cross explains it well. He says that what is happening in this dark night is that God

> *transfers His goods and strength from sense to spirit. Since the sensory part of the soul is incapable of the goods of the spirit, it remains deprived, dry, and empty, and thus, while the spirit is tasting, the flesh tastes nothing at all and becomes weak in its work. But the spirit through this nourishment grows stronger and more alert and becomes more solicitous than before about not failing God.[2]*

The passage may be difficult to grasp at first, since John implies that only the senses are in darkness, whereas the spirit "all the time is being fed." If this is so, why are we not aware of this food of the spirit? Why is it that everything seems dark to us and we have no sense at all that God is transferring to the spirit the good things of the senses? Why does it seem to us that God is totally absent and we are lost? John is quite aware of these questions, for he goes on to say: "If (the spirit) is not immediately conscious of spiritual sweetness and delight, but only of aridity and lack of sweetness, the reason for this is . . . (because) its palate has been accustomed to those other sensual pleasures upon which its eyes are still fixed." The spirit has no taste for the things of the Spirit because its taste is only accustomed to the things of this earth. Thus, it looks for the only things it knows—the delights of sense—and when these are absent it feels that everything is lost.

John's explanation implies that the darkness is not really darkness, that God is not really absent, but that we lack the eyes to see, the tongue to taste what is really there. That is precisely his point. God is not absent; he is closer than he has ever been, but we are blind. It is this dark contemplation which is in us, working our healing. For some time it will appear to us that we are doing nothing at prayer, and in one sense we are right: We are indeed doing nothing at the natural level of sense and intellect and feeling, the level on which we have always lived and the only level we know. That is why we can say that from our natural point of view our prayer at this time is simply a question of learning to do nothing, to waste time gracefully. It is perhaps the hardest thing we ever learn to do, and not everyone who comes to this point in prayer succeeds in adjusting to the apparent vacuum. Many fill the void with their own activities, whether these be novenas or meditations or extra apostolic works. They find the uncertainty, the letting go, too much to accept; they have "many possessions" and they go away sad when the Lord tells them to give away all they possess (their own ideas, plans, control of the situation) and come follow him. They create their own piety, their own spirituality, and I am sure the Lord loves them for it, but how poor a substitute it is for the wonders he would work in them, if only they were able, in times of prayer, to let go of everything and give him a free hand in their lives!

This is not to say that we should abandon our apostolic and family responsibilities. They continue (sometimes joyfully), even when our prayer becomes dark—though they, too, may sometimes be part of the purifying darkness in that they lose their savor and seem peculiarly unfulfilling. In the Epilogue I will say more about this latter experience as part of the dark night in the active, apostolic life.

• • •

The Log Becoming Fire

As we have seen (chapter 2, note 5) John of the Cross distinguishes two dark nights: that of the senses, which "is common to many," and that of the spirit, which "is the lot of very few."[3] Both nights are actually the infused contemplation of which we spoke in chapter 4, working its purification in us. But as this fire of God's love penetrates our being its effects are felt deeper and deeper in us. At first the fire chars and blackens the surface of the wood, and this corresponds to the darkening of the senses and faculties of which we have been speaking. But as the heat penetrates deeper and deeper into the heart of the log, the same fire which effected the charring of the surface now begins to transform the very substance of the wood, until the whole log is incandescent and, in the physics of John's day, the wood becomes fire.[4] The image expresses beautifully the divinization of the soul effected by the penetrating fire of infused contemplation. It is a transformation which the soul, the log, could never bring about by itself or by its own efforts.

But why does John say that the night of sense is common and comes to many who are serious about prayer, whereas the night of the spirit is the lot of very few? It cannot be because the Lord has set different limits to the growth of different persons, since John says that it is the very same fire of contemplation which works these two effects in us. Moreover, it would scarcely make sense for the Lord to intend merely to char and blacken the wood (the night of the senses) and then to leave it forever in that deformed state. It is true that he alone determines the pace of the transformation he wishes to work in us, but the whole purpose of the charring is that the log may become fire, that the soul may become divine. The God who loved us enough to give his only-begotten Son for us cannot possibly desire any less than this. As we have seen earlier, Jesus makes this very clear in the Last Supper discourse (especially Jn 14:15–24), and John's first epistle (3:2) is emphatic on the point.

The reason, then, why so few in this life pass from the night of sense to the night of spirit must be sought in our response to the fire of contemplation working in us. When the log begins to be all charred and blackened, when the cracks and knotholes all begin to be magnified by the fire's work and all the maggots in the wood are driven out to the surface, the log appears far uglier than before. If the log could think, it would say to itself: This is a disaster! My desire to become fire was a terrible mistake. I am much worse off now than when I started. It would seek to escape from the fire before everything was lost.

Similarly, the closer the soul comes to the light of God, the darker its own darkness appears by contrast. It feels that it is getting worse and moving farther from God, because all the hidden cracks and worms are seen in stark contrast to the holiness of God. The problem is that the soul can think and can seek to escape from the disaster of the fire's burning, whereas the log of wood cannot. The soul can lose its

nerve, get discouraged, fear the pain of the divine fire, especially if it is not truly open to a good director who can properly interpret what is really happening. Thus, it can abort
the transformation God is seeking to accomplish. Since the
Lord always respects our freedom and never forces himself
on us, it is possible for us to set limits to his work in us.
John felt that most sincere pray-ers do precisely this, and as
a result few of them are fully penetrated by the fire of God
in this life. It is a sad state, to be charred and blackened and
thus spoiled for the decorative uses of natural wood and yet
not really be hot enough to catch fire. We are left suspended
between earth and heaven!

• • •

How Can We Respond Gracefully?

Since none of us, as far as I know, ever passes this critical
point easily and with a light heart, we are all in this sad,
suspended state at least for a time—and probably quite a
long time. How can we respond gracefully when we find
ourselves in such an unnatural situation? How can we cooperate fully with the Lord working in us, so that the charring
of the wood may gradually give way to the incandescence
of the divine fire in us? We have already seen, at the end of
chapter 4, that John advises us to do just two things: first,
to have a good director and trust the Lord to speak to us
through him or her; that is, to live in faith that we are on the
right road, despite all contrary appearances, unless and until
the director judges that we have lost our way. Second, to
abandon all attempts to meditate or to reach God ourselves
and simply "allow the soul to remain in rest and quietude,
even though it may seem very obvious to them that they
are doing nothing and wasting time. . . . Through patience
and perseverance in prayer they will be doing a great deal
without activity on their part."[5]

The problem is that this situation becomes the normal pattern of our prayer life for a long period of time. The darkness and the doing nothing begin to wear on our nerves, and we begin to doubt whether God is really working. Are we perhaps just deceiving ourselves? Our patience wears thin, and the devil sees an opening to sow the seeds of doubt and to spoil the work the Lord is doing in darkness. Even the director, as St. John of the Cross says, seems not to be much help to us at this time, because we begin to doubt whether he is being too optimistic. Perhaps he does not really understand our inner sinfulness, our real situation before the all holy God. The real problem, as the darkness becomes more and more the usual pattern of our prayer, is that we feel we are really getting worse and that God is farther away from us than ever.

As the log sees all the darkness and ugliness in itself, sees the cracks and knotholes and maggots which were previously concealed from it, it almost inevitably thinks (since this log that is the soul can think) that it is far worse than it was before, when all of these defects were invisible. We have said in chapter 2 that one of the principal flowers in the garden of the Lord is an awareness of our own sinfulness. But now we feel that this painful awareness is an ugly weed rather than a flower and that the Lord of the garden could never take his delight in such a place.

John of the Cross points out that this is one of the greatest sufferings of the soul that advances into the depths of the dark night. Any encouraging word from the director seems clearly contradictory to what the soul actually feels, and thus must be mistaken.

> Added to this, because of the solitude and desolation this night causes, is the fact that a person in this state finds neither consolation nor support in any doctrine or spiritual director. Although his

143

*spiritual director may point out many reasons for
being comforted on account of the blessings con-
tained in these afflictions, he cannot believe this.
Because he is engulfed and immersed in that sen-
timent of evils by which he so clearly sees his own
miseries, he believes his directors say these things
because they do not understand him and do not
see what he sees and feels. Instead of consolation
he experiences greater sorrow thinking that the
director's doctrine is no remedy for his evil.*[6]

• • •

Surrendering Even Our Sinfulness

John goes on to say that the soul is right in judging
this way! That is, the soul will receive little comfort in its
feelings from the words of the director at a time like this,
since the darkness has completely penetrated its feelings.
But I believe we can offer some advice which will help the
soul to understand its misery and to survive the darkness.
In the first place, this misery is clearly a case of desolation,
anxiety, turmoil, loss of faith, hope, love, peace—and St.
Ignatius tells us that such desolation can never be the voice
of God for one who is seeking him. Thus the cardinal principle is never to make or change a decision at such times. We
should never trust our judgment of what God is doing, or
how we stand before him, when that judgment is formed in
desolation. We discussed in chapter 3 the reasons why the
Lord permits the evil spirit to assail us with desolation. By
this stage in its dark journey, the soul will be quite familiar
with all those reasons, although they may provide it with
no more relief than the words of the director. But the crucial
thing is simply to refuse to trust the judgments about myself and God which are born of desolation. We must simply

hang on by our teeth and continue to call upon the name of the Lord until the desolation passes.

It seems to me that there is also something deeper which we can say about such a situation. As I have reflected on it over the years, I have come to believe that the true root of our anguish is the difficulty we have in really letting go of ourselves. This trial is part of the whole process of allowing the Lord to be more and more the Lord of our lives. John of the Cross says somewhere that we first encounter God in our own sinfulness, and only secondly in creatures, and only lastly in himself—a statement which my own experience as a director has led me to believe is profoundly true. Yet, paradoxically, I have also become convinced that our own sinfulness is the very last thing we surrender to the Lord. Even when we have truly allowed him to be the Lord of our lives, there is the residual conviction that "my sins at least are my own," that when I come face to face with the Lord of love, the one thing I have which I have not been given is my sinfulness, my failure to love. This is true, of course, in the sense that our refusal to love can never be caused by Love himself. Yet, even the wounds of our lovelessness must be—can only be—healed by him. Even the fact of my sinfulness is something which only he can transform. The passive purification of the soul which John calls the "dark night" means that, beyond the point of transition from the active "ascent of Mount Carmel" to the passive "dark night of the soul," the work of purification is wholly God's work, and my contribution is to give him full freedom to accomplish his transformation in me.[7]

If the soul in darkness can begin to realize that this is what is happening, it can see its painful experience of sinfulness and separation from God in an entirely new way. All the ugliness that is made manifest must simply be placed in the hands of God. My sinfulness is to be surrendered to the Lord, not to be anguished over as if there were something

145

I could do about it if only I could find the right formula, or as if my inability to do anything about it is an occasion for despair. It is the last dark part of myself which I place, perhaps out of desperation, wholly in the transforming hands of the Lord.

• • •

Two Clouds: Unknowing and Forgetting

Another of the great masters of prayer is the unknown author of the *Cloud of Unknowing*. He was an Englishman who lived in the fourteenth century, and composed his brief work for a "dear friend in God" who is one "of those who feel the mysterious action of the Spirit in their inmost being stirring them to love. I do not say that they continually feel this stirring, as experienced contemplatives do, but now and again they taste something of contemplative love in the very core of their being."[8] In the final chapter the author gives signs by which we may know whether we are called to contemplation. And a close examination of these signs makes clear that the "cloud of unknowing" of which the author speaks is essentially the same experience as that which John calls the "dark night." Many scholars, in fact, have noted the striking similarity of the Cloud to St. John of the Cross and have questioned whether John, writing two hundred years later, was influenced by the doctrine of the Cloud.[9] The question is difficult to answer, but this much is certain: In spite of the gap of the centuries and the even wider gulf of temperament between John, the fiery Castilian who is perhaps the greatest poet Spain has ever produced, and the dry, ironic Englishman whose descriptions of the enemies of contemplation have a real sarcastic bite to them[10]—despite these differences, it is clear that it is the same Lord working the same wondrous mystery of contemplation in these two great persons.

We said above that the soul in the dark night can be helped if it is aware of the fact that this experience is desolation, and resolves never to make a decision in the throes of desolation; and, further, if it begins to see this desolation as due to our reluctance to surrender even our sinfulness into the healing hands of God, who alone must determine the time and the manner of our healing. I have introduced the *Cloud of Unknowing* at this point because I believe its author also has some very helpful positive guidance to offer the soul in this state of desolating darkness. The title of the book is his description of such a soul vis-à-vis God: The Lord we seek is enveloped in a cloud of unknowing which the mind of the pray-er cannot penetrate. All our thoughts and images of God fall far short of the reality. Hence, as we draw closer, or are drawn closer, to the All-Holy, nothing we can think or say seems to have any value in imaging or expressing our experience. All the words of our favorite prayers, which previously enabled us to "remember with joy," now seem like ashes in our mouths. What can we do? How should we respond in the face of an experience beyond thoughts and words?

The author of the Cloud says, in essence, that when this becomes our experience in prayer we must respond by accepting the cloud of unknowing above us and by fashioning a cloud of forgetting beneath us. These two clouds, one of which we passively experience and the other of which we labor to produce, comprise the whole doctrine on contemplative prayer of the *Cloud of Unknowing*. The author reveals himself as a consummate teacher, matching utter simplicity to rare depth of insight. Toward the beginning of the book, he summarizes its content in this way:

> *This is what you are to do (when the Lord leads you to this more passive, darker way of prayer): lift your heart up to the Lord, with a gentle stirring of*

*love desiring him for his own sake and not for his
gifts. Center all your attention and desire on him
and let this be the sole concern of your mind and
heart. Do all in your power to forget everything
else, keeping your thoughts and desires free from
any of God's creatures or their affairs whether in
general or in particular. Perhaps this will seem
like an irresponsible attitude, but I tell you, let
them all be; pay no attention to them. What I
am describing here is the contemplative work of
the spirit. It is this which gives God the greatest
delight. . . . Your fellow men are marvelously
enriched by this work of yours, even if you may
not fully understand how.[11]*

● ● ●

When to Waste Time Gracefully

We could scarcely express more clearly what I meant
earlier in saying we must learn to waste time gracefully. We
must center totally on God himself, "for his own sake and
not for his gifts," and we must "do all in (our) power to forget everything else." The problem is not in understanding
the doctrine of the Cloud but in accepting it, and in this it
perfectly mirrors the demands of God's contemplative work
in us. As the author says, this letting go of everything else
"will seem like an irresponsible attitude" to the Christian
living in a world in need of redemption, and never more so
than today when justice and faith are seen as so intimately
connected in the Christian life. How can I forget everything
else and still be a follower of the Christ who came to preach
the gospel to the poor, to bind up the brokenhearted? How
genuine is a spirituality which leads me to neglect the basic
human needs of my neighbor?

As long as the question is posed that way, we will never grasp the meaning and salvific value of this dark contemplation. Yet, how else can it be posed? If there is another way of seeing things, it is certainly not a natural way; even the author of the Cloud admits this when he says it will seem like "an irresponsible attitude." His point, however, is that the one whom God has led to this point can no longer rely on the natural ways of seeing and understanding. Note, however, that the author of the Cloud is speaking here of one who can no longer meditate as she could before. This is one of the main signs he gives that the pray-er is ready for the doctrine of the *Cloud of Unknowing*. He is not recommending "centering prayer" to beginners; he says, in fact, that his little book should not be given to them. But when God provides a "cloud of unknowing," then the pray-er must learn to view things from an entirely different, a divine perspective.

In chapter 6 we will have to try to describe this divine perspective. But for now let us ask: What precisely must we bury beneath this cloud of forgetting? The author of the Cloud tells us: "Assuming that you have done your best to amend your life according to the laws of the Church" (one of the essential works of the beginner in prayer . . . see chapter 5 of *Opening to God*), and assuming that the Lord himself has led you to passivity, contemplation,

> if the memory of your past sins or the temptation
> to new ones should plague your mind, forming an
> obstacle between you and God . . . try to bury the
> thought of these deeds beneath the thick cloud of
> forgetting just as if neither you nor anyone else
> had ever done them. If they persist in returning,
> you must persist in rejecting them. In short, as
> often as they rise up you must put them down.[12]

Our sinful past must be buried under this cloud of forgetting; as we said earlier, even this sinfulness must be wholly entrusted to the Lord. Many pious, elderly people are tormented in old age by worry about their past. Such worry may seem sincerely devout, but it is really a delusion and a snare. Their eyes should be wholly on the merciful Lord and all such concerns should be buried beneath this cloud of forgetting.

So, too, should all speculation about God and his works, all seeking for insights and deeper understanding.

> *This is why I urge you to dismiss every clever or subtle thought, no matter how holy or valuable. Cover it over with a thick cloud of forgetting because in this life only love can touch God as he is in himself, never knowledge. As long as we live in these mortal bodies the keenness of our intellect remains dulled by material limitations whenever it deals with spiritual realities and most especially God.*[13]

We mentioned earlier that we should no longer seek to labor with our intellects and imaginations once our prayer becomes contemplative. The author of the Cloud goes even further and says we should even dismiss such insights if they come spontaneously.

The question that has come to me with respect to his advice is this: What if the insights are from the Lord? Might I not be rejecting his way of working? The answer, I think, is that we can quite safely follow the advice of the Cloud, since our human tendency will be to be too active mentally, and by working against this tendency we are much more likely to strike the proper balance of dynamic receptivity. If it is the Lord really working through our thoughts, he will persist despite our attempts to dismiss them. If, as is much more likely, it is our own minds seeking to insert themselves into the contemplative work, these insights will usually fade away once we seriously seek to dismiss them. Thus I have found it quite safe, and pleasing to the Lord, to say to him: "Lord, if these thoughts and images are really from you, you insist on them. But since it is more likely that I am the source of them and they are interfering with your work in me, I will continue quietly to push them aside." Usually that is the end of them—at least for the moment!

• • •

Forgetting All Except God

The author of the Cloud also says that we must "forget all about time, place and matter in this spiritual work."[14] In short, we must empty our mind and heart of everything except God.

> *Reject the knowledge and experience of everything less than God, treading it all down beneath the cloud of forgetting. And now also you must learn to forget not only every creature and its deeds but yourself as well, along with whatever you may have accomplished in God's service. For a true lover not only cherishes his beloved more than himself but in a certain sense he becomes oblivious of himself on account of the one he loves.[15]*

It is important to recall that this forgetting of everything except God differs from the great Oriental prayer traditions in one important respect: For the author of the Cloud, as for John of the Cross, we should never seek to empty our minds, to forget every creature, unless and until it is clear that God is leading us to contemplation. That is, until the three signs of the dark night (which we discussed at the end of chapter 4) are verified in our own prayer experience. The advice of the Cloud is essentially the same, although John's guidelines are much more specific. Until this time, meditation and reflection—on the gospels, on our own sinful situation, on the needs of our brethren—are not only proper but necessary in our prayer. It is important to remember this in evaluating the various centering prayer movements today. Some pray-ers (including myself!) have merely caused themselves anxiety and frustration by trying to anticipate the Lord and leap into the cloud of forgetting on their own initiative.

When John's three signs are verified, however, the Cloud of Forgetting is the only appropriate response to what the Lord is doing in us. If he makes it dark, we must seek to allow it to be even darker! Rather than seeking to return to the natural light by which we have previously lived, we must embrace the darkness and positively cooperate with the work of the Spirit in us. That this is laborious and painful is without question. But once we are called to it, it promises a reward (and an apostolic effectiveness) beyond our imagining. As the author of the Cloud says:

> The labor, of course, is in the unrelenting struggle to banish the countless distracting thoughts that plague our minds and to restrain them beneath that cloud of forgetting which I spoke of earlier. This is the suffering. All the struggle is on man's side in the effort he must make to prepare himself for God's action, which is the awakening of love and which he alone can do. But persevere in doing your part and I promise you that God will not fail to do his.[16]

From time to time the Lord gives us hints of this "awakening of love." He lets us begin to realize "how wonderfully is a man's love transformed by the interior experience of this nothingness and this nowhere. . . . He who patiently abides in this darkness will be comforted and feel again a confidence about his destiny, for gradually he will see his past sins healed by grace. The pain continues, yet he knows it will end, for even now it grows less intense."[17] In chapter 6 I hope to say something, insofar as I am able, about the new confidence and apostolic effectiveness which are the fruit of this dark transformation of love. It is important to realize now, however, that once it begins we live in this darkness all of our lives. "Even those innocent of grave sin will spend their whole lives at this work because as long as we are in these mortal bodies we shall experience the impenetrable darkness of the cloud of unknowing between us and God."[18]

• • •

Joyful Enthusiasm Even in Purgatory

"I never promised you a rose garden!" Any good director must be able to say that to those whose journey to the dark places he has been privileged to share. Like John of the Cross, the author of the *Cloud of Unknowing* identifies this journey with purgatory. Yet, this identification is not really as gloomy or as frightening as it might seem to be at first. For purgatory, after all, is not an end, an endless state, but a means to transformation and eternal life. To discover that prayer beyond the beginnings is purgatory is to discover that it is not (at least not yet) heaven, as we hoped and expected. But it is also to discover that it is not hell! As the Cloud puts it, "Slowly he begins to realize that the suffering he endures is really not hell at all, but his purgatory."[19] For one who has truly begun to love the Lord above all things, and to desire only him, this realization, once fully grasped, is joy enough to sustain her on the purgatory journey.

After my experience at the Naga Carmel, when I realized that I myself was much more secure in the dark, my whole attitude towards the dark night, the cloud of unknowing, was changed. Gradually I came to be at home in the dark, even though I knew it could never be a permanent home. I realized what it meant to desire that the Lord do his transforming work at his own pace, since he really does know what is best for us. As the years passed and I began to realize that the fear of darkness was slowly (all too slowly!) fading away, a new realization took root: Once we no longer fear the dark, what is there that we could possibly fear? Everything is safe in the gentle, healing hands of the Lord, our Love.

In one of his most beautiful chapters, the author of the Cloud says:

> For the love of God, then, be careful and do not imprudently strain yourself in this work. Rely more on joyful enthusiasm than on sheer brute force . . . avoid all unnatural compulsion and learn to love joyfully with a sweet and gentle disposition of body and soul. Wait with gracious and modest courtesy for the Lord's initiative.[20]

This joyful enthusiasm, this waiting with gracious and modest courtesy, is, I suspect, characteristic of purgatory itself and is the guarantee of purgatory's own ending. That is why purgatory is not hell, whether we live it here or hereafter!

6

To Know the Place
for the First Time

• • •

Most people, in my experience, are not very good at floating. Filipinos, who live on several hundred islands surrounded by the ocean—who should, one would think, be much at home in the sea—are no better at it than others. In fact, it is always surprising to me how few Filipinos really know how to swim, or even to float. As a result, I have spent a good bit of my time on picnics teaching or trying to teach the students to float. I'm a polar bear from northern New York where summers are brief, if indeed they come at all, and those few short weeks of summer weather were the golden time of the year. Lake Ontario was a magnet to which I was drawn whenever the days were warm and about which I dreamt during the long cold months. Here in the Philippines, however, where it is summer the whole year round, and where the sea is never more than an hour away, we take it for granted. Like the Statue of Liberty for New Yorkers, or the Golden Gate Bridge for San Franciscans, the sea is so constantly present that we scarcely notice it. Amazingly, I swim less often here than I did in New York!

Maybe this is why I have been struck by the mystery of floating. When we do have a picnic and I try to teach these people of the sea how to float, it is puzzling to see what a difficult art floating really is—difficult not because it demands much skill, but because it demands much letting go. The secret of floating is in learning not to do all the things we instinctively want to do. We want to keep ourselves rigid, ready to save ourselves the moment a big wave comes along, and yet the more rigid we are the more likely we are to be swamped by the waves. If we relax in the water we can be carried up and down by the rolling sea and never be swamped. We want to keep our heads out of the water to avoid having our noses and mouths filled with the sea, but the more we raise our heads, the more likely we are to be unbalanced and to end up with a noseful of water. If we can persuade ourselves to put our heads back, to rest on the water as on a pillow, we don't sink; we float! Once we have discovered this by experience, floating is never difficult again. It seems so easy now that we find it hard to imagine why we ever thought it difficult. We are at home in the sea.

Yet, many people never learn how to float. They never manage to take the initial risk, to do the opposite of what their instincts tell them. They never learn to relax, to let their head be pillowed by the water, to let go, hang loose, float free. Perhaps they simply decide they don't want to take the risk. They make their choice to be "landlubbers," and they busy themselves on the shore with all the amusements they can enjoy without getting their feet wet. If they are honest, they occasionally gaze wistfully at the sea and the floaters and think what might have been for them—if only they could take the risk. But if they are foolish, they turn their backs resolutely to the sea and gradually, as the land alone fills their gaze over the years, convince themselves that the sea is a mirage for those foolish enough to look in the opposite direction, that there is no such thing as floating, that the distant voices of the floaters behind them are really no voices at all.

There are, however, some courageous souls who do want to learn how to float, and who look around for someone in the water to teach them. But what does it mean to "teach" floating? If all it entailed was a brief explanation about relaxing your body and letting your head lie back in the water, it seems that everyone would be a floater and everyone a teacher. But that is obviously not true. Learning to float is counterintuitive: we have to do the very opposite of what our self-preserving instincts urge us to do. The good teacher is the one who can inspire confidence in us, whom we trust enough to do the opposite of what our instincts urge, simply because she says it is the right thing to do. It is not at all hard to do these things, but it is very hard to believe that we will be safe in doing them. The good teacher inspires this belief, this trust, because we see her doing successfully what she urges us to do, and because we know by experience that she would not deceive us or trick us. Practical jokers may have a place in the scheme of creation, but they will never teach anyone to float! People learn to float when they trust me enough to be confident that I will not play a trick on them, when they feel sure that my hands under their back and under their legs are as steady and as sure as dry land, that my hands will not be suddenly removed without warning, that, when they are removed, they will never be far away, ready to provide support whenever needed. To learn to float, it seems, is essentially to learn to trust, first the teacher and then the water.

Learning to "Float" in the Dark

Toward the end of chapter 5 I spoke of learning to be at home in the dark. I said that this gradual coming to be at home is perhaps the crucial turning point in the life of contemplative prayer. It means, in terms of floating, that we have learned to be at home in the sea that is God, with no visible means of support except the water whose ebb and flow, whose sudden surgings, we cannot predict or control.

If you recall, I began the epilogue of *Opening to God* with the story of a sister-friend who attended my course on prayer. At the end of the course she said, "I have found it very fruitful. But I was hoping you would say something about the goal of the interior life—where it is all leading." I took her to mean the more exalted experience of unitive prayer about which St. Teresa speaks in the latter mansions of the *Interior Castle* and St. John of the Cross in the *Spiritual Canticle* and the *Living Flame of Love*. I knew I had very little to say about that ultimate goal, at least if what I said was going to be true to my own experience.[1] Moreover, as I explained in the epilogue, I felt that this was not the goal which should preoccupy us. What we should be concerned about is letting God become the absolute Lord of our lives. This is the real goal which we should set before ourselves, and this is the goal toward which he works in the whole of our interior lives. That was the central point of the epilogue of *Opening to God*, and it is the whole point of *When the Well Runs Dry*. This book is simply an expansion and development of the same insight.

In the two years that have passed since I wrote *Opening to God*, I have often thought of my sister-friend's question about the "goal of it all." I feel that I would still give the same answer as I gave then. The image of floating has come to dominate my thinking about prayer more and more, because it seems to capture perfectly for me the goal towards

159

which the whole purifying process of the dark night is leading us. If we want to reach a goal that we ourselves have chosen, we would be well advised to learn to swim rather than to float. The swimmer is intensely active and is going someplace; the floater yields to the flow of the water and savors fully being where he is. He, too, is going someplace, but that is the concern of the current which carries him. His major decision is whether to trust the tide. If he does not, he must guide himself by his swimming strokes; if he does, he can relax and surrender himself totally to the tide, and live fully the present moment.

The problem is that we must decide whether we want to swim or to float.

• • •

God Wants Total Floating

Most of us want to do a bit of both. When we tire of swimming we like to float, but when our floating carries us beyond the safe zone, then we swim again to get back where we are secure. It seems, however, that we cannot do both together forever. The whole experience of the dark night or the cloud of unknowing appears to be the Lord's way of trying to make floaters out of swimmers. He, it seems, definitely wishes us to float. He wants us to have as our goal our total surrender to the flow of this tide. He has another goal, it is true. He is leading us somewhere; our floating is not to be an endless, directionless circling in a fathomless sea. But that is his goal; he would like us to trust him enough to relax, to leave the goal wholly to him, and to concretize our trust by savoring fully the expanse of sky and sea which is open to our gaze now. Only those who are totally secure in their love can live thus fully the present moment. Only those who have forgotten themselves completely, who truly float free, can give their whole voice to blessing the wind and the wave.

This freedom of spirit and joy in the gifts of the present moment which characterize the floater correspond closely to the advice which John of the Cross gives to souls experiencing the dark night. As we pointed out at the end of chapter 4, he says: "Through patience and perseverance in prayer, they will be doing a great deal without activity on their part. Content simply with a loving and peaceful attentiveness to God, and live without the concern, without the effort, and without desire to taste or feel Him."[2] When the dark night is a new experience, this advice is very difficult to understand. During all our prayer lives we have been swimmers, accustomed to travel toward God by the strenuous efforts of our own faculties. When John tells us we will now travel faster by simply floating—doing nothing and desiring nothing— it is difficult even to imagine how he could be correct. If we do accept his advice, it is not because we are convinced of its reasonableness, but because we find ourselves exhausted by our own efforts and incapable of doing anything else.

When we have learned to float and to be at home doing nothing, we can see by our own experience the rightness of John's counsel. We still do not understand the mystery of floating, and almost inevitably there will be moments of self-doubt when we wonder whether our whole prayer life may be an illusion, or whether perhaps we are "just lazy." In our better moments, though, we know by experience that we are right to float, and we realize that the doubts are due to the fact that we now live in the cloud of unknowing, in the darkness of faith, where we cannot possibly see with our natural faculties what God is doing. We are filled with that new confidence, dark but strong, of which we spoke at the end of chapter 5.

This new confidence is itself the immediate, proximate goal of the whole experience of the dark night. It is a total, unquestioning trust that God is God, that he does love us more than we love ourselves, and that he is truly working in us to bring to perfection the good work he has begun in us. It is the trust of the child in his father, unquestioning and unconditional even though the father's intentions are totally mysterious to the child. This attitude of trust is the heart of the spirituality of the Little Flower, St. Thérèse of Lisieux. Her "little way" is the only way there is. She herself seems not to have realized this, since she tells us that she came to the "little way" only because she felt that the heroic way of the saints was too difficult for her. Since she could not do great things for God, she would have to find her holiness in the simple love of a child for her Father—not in doing but in letting him do everything in and for her. Thérèse died in 1897 at the age of twenty-four, and was canonized less than thirty years later[3]—remarkably quickly for a church which usually acts with extreme caution in evaluating the lives and virtues of candidates for sainthood. The reason, I believe, is because her "little way" is really the gospel way and perfectly embodies the disposition of anyone who has truly learned the ways of God. We begin by desiring to do great things for him, but we discover, by the darkness of the cloud of unknowing, that "he who is mighty" does all the great things, for us as he did for Mary (Lk 1:49). He has looked upon our lowliness; his name is holy forever. Although Thérèse does not seem to have lived long enough to realize it, her "little way" is the only way possible. The remarkable thing is that she realized so quickly for herself what most of us discover only by a lifetime of darkness.

• • •

What Happens When We Do Float?

What happens when we discover and accept the meaning of floating free, of leaving everything to God? It would be nice to be able to say that this discovery means the end of darkness. But that is not true, because the darkness of prayer is not simply due to our own reluctance to float. In a deeper sense, it is "dark" because our minds simply cannot grasp God in this life. As long as we are in the body, our ways of knowing and feeling are embodied ways, finite ways—ways which can never adequately embrace the infinite God. St. Paul says: "Now I see only reflections in a mirror, mere riddles, but then we shall be seeing face to face. Now I can only know imperfectly; but then I shall know just as fully as I am myself known" (1 Cor 13:12). In this life our knowledge of God is inevitably imperfect, indistinct, since the Lord we love is one "whose home is in inaccessible light, whom no human being has seen or is able to see" (1 Tim 6:16; see Jn 1:18; 6:46; 1 Jn 4:12). The life of the dark night does engender in us an aching desire for God, but the fulfillment of that desire can only come when we are "dissolved" to be with Christ. This is why death becomes for us, as for Paul (2 Cor 5:1–10), not a horror to be fled from but a consummation devoutly to be wished.

This surprising inversion of our natural way of viewing death is significant. While we do not escape the darkness once we learn to float free in the sea of God, something very important does happen to our ways of knowing and judging. At root we can say that we discover that we are at home in the dark and, as I said earlier, we find that we no longer fear the darkness, the very darkness which caused us such anxiety and inner turmoil in the past. It is not that we are satisfied with this dark cloud of unknowing; our desire for the light that is God grows stronger with every passing day. But it is not an anxious desire. We are secure in the darkness, obscurely but strongly confident that we are in the hands of a God who cares for us totally and will infallibly work his will in us if only we continue to trust. Darkness is no longer a threat, but a promise and a cause of joy. With this comes an inversion of all our customary ways of seeing and valuing. While we cannot yet see God in himself, we do begin to see the world and ourselves through God's eyes.[4] Everything, it seems, appears in a new light and at times we are like a child under the tree on Christmas morning.

T. S. Eliot has described the experience in one of my favorite poetic passages:

> With the drawing of this Love and the voice of this Calling
> We shall not cease from exploration,
> And the end of all our exploring
> Will be to arrive where we started
> And know the place for the first time.
>> Four Quartets
>> Little Gidding, V

The love of God is a magnet drawing us ever beyond our present situation. God is always just out of reach, far enough away so we can never settle down in comfortable complacency, and yet never so far that we give up the quest as hopeless—once we can abandon our own expectations and let him truly be the Lord of the dance, the Master of the hunt. As we explore further and further we gradually begin to discover that the Lord is leading us, not into some strange angelic world, but deeper and deeper into the heart of our very concrete existence. For the Zen Buddhist, the Buddha divinity is ordinary life, "three pounds of flax," three kilos of rice. While this cannot mean for us Christians that God is simply identical with his creation, there is something profoundly and paradoxically true about the Zen insight. The interior life is not so much a flight to the stars as a journey deeper and deeper into the very center of ourselves, to the core of our being where God alone dwells and where we have never been. It seems to me that this is one of the central insights of St. John's gospel: The interior life is not a question of seeing extraordinary things, but rather of seeing the ordinary things with the eyes of God.

Thus it is true, as Eliot said, that the end of all our exploring will be to arrive where we started and know the place for the first time. This has been beautifully confirmed many times in my life as a director. How often good souls have exclaimed to me, when once they began to realize how God was really working in their lives, "How blind I have been! How foolish! I thought all was lost, and I never realized what the Lord was doing. Only now do I begin to see that he has been closer to me than I to myself." They have discovered, to their chagrin, that God has not been absent as they thought all along. He has been present, and it is they who have been absent from him. They have been blinded by his light, and now they realize that darkness is light, that death is life, that failure is success and success failure.

Like the disciples on the road to Emmaus, they had been hoping, and all their hopes seemed shattered by the Lord's disastrous death. When he came up and walked along the road, their eyes were blinded and they could not recognize him. They even told him of all their broken dreams, without ever realizing that he, about whom they were speaking with such sadness, was the very one they were speaking to! He finally said to them: "You foolish men! So slow to believe all that the prophets have said! Was it not necessary that the Christ should suffer before entering into his glory?" (Lk 24:25–26). Even then, as he went on to interpret for them the things in the Old Testament concerning himself, they still did not recognize him. Their healing was very gradual, as God's ways always seem to be. But something was kindled in their hearts as he spoke. It was a faint flame of hope which led them to urge him, still unrecognized, to stay with them for supper when they reached Emmaus. Of course, he accepted. Their invitation, freely and insistently offered, was the one thing he greatly desired, and the only thing they could contribute to the miracle of his return to them. He would never force himself on them, just as he will never force himself on us. But after they had listened "while their hearts were burning within them," he was more eager to stay with them than they were to have him. At long last they could recognize him, in the simplest and most human of gestures, a gesture they had seen so many times before, a gesture which he had used just three days previously as a dramatic symbol of his love for them: When he had seated himself with them to eat, he took bread, pronounced the blessing, then broke the bread and began to distribute it to them. With that their eyes were opened and they recognized him (Lk 24:30–31).

What a moment that must have been! It is difficult even to imagine how they felt unless we have known both their sense of loss and the wonder of the Lord's return. Shortly after this incident Jesus appeared to the 11 apostles and their companions in the upper room in Jerusalem. He showed them his hands and feet, to prove to them that it was really he. St. Luke, in a phrase of which only he was capable, tells us that they "disbelieved for sheer joy" (Lk 24:41). It is an extraordinary statement; for me, one of the most beautiful in all scripture. What kind of unbelief is this? Certainly not the kind to be censured, regretted. It is the unbelief of a wife when she learns that her beloved husband, who she had been told had died in battle, suddenly turns up alive and returns to her. It is the unbelief I saw on the face of my father when I, whom he had never expected to see again, stood suddenly by his deathbed in the hospital. "I can't believe it!" We do believe of course, but the joy is so far beyond all our hopes and expectations that we are struck dumb with wonder.

The Resurrection in Our Life

Can we ever feel that way about the Lord? Only if we, too, have loved and apparently lost him as they did. This is precisely the deeper meaning of the dark night. Absence does make the heart grow fonder, for those who have truly come to share a loving presence. It is, in fact, in absence that we come to realize how completely the Lord has come to be at the very center of our lives, and how totally we have come to depend on him. When he returns to us, when we "return where we started and know the place for the first time," it is a totally new experience. "I never realized! I never knew! How blind I was!" He is, mysteriously, the same Lord we have long known, and yet he is totally different. Our experience is much like that of the disciples at Easter who did not dare to ask him who he was, because "they knew it was the Lord" (Jn 21:12). We, too, when at last the anguished absence of the dark night comes to an end in our personal Easter experience, are face to face with the beauty, ever ancient yet ever new, of which St. Augustine spoke so wonderingly. In my experience as a director, this happens suddenly and without warning: In fact, it seems that it happens only when we have all but given up hope of ever knowing the Lord's loving touch again.

This giving up of hope, though, is a profoundly mysterious reality. To the soul it seems very close to despair, but in truth it is also very far—infinitely far—from despair. Very close in the sense that the soul does have the feeling, as John of the Cross puts it, "that all is now over for it (i.e. that its situation is hopeless and God has abandoned it) and that it will never again be happy as in the past."[5] At the same time, though, the soul, without realizing it or even being able to believe it, is very far from despair. Despair means giving up: giving up hope, giving up the search for God, giving up, if possible, the desire for God. Yet, the very darkness which seems so hopeless has been working precisely the opposite effects in the soul, without the person's ever guessing it. When John of the Cross enumerates the benefits which this dark night is accomplishing in the soul whom the Lord leads into it, he mentions especially the following: the knowledge of oneself and one's misery; a greater respect and courtesy in communing with God; a knowledge of the greatness and excellence of God; spiritual humility; the love of its neighbors ("he will esteem them and not judge them as he did before, when he was aware that he enjoyed an intense fervor while others did not"!); submission and obedience to direction.[6]

If the only effects were a deep realization of my own misery and of God's incomprehensible grandeur, the result might well be despair. But despair is really a perverse form of vanity—an unwillingness to accept and to live with my misery, a refusal to hope, born of wounded pride. Humility, submission to direction, an esteem of others as better than myself, all these fruits of the genuine dark night are directly opposed to the wounded pride which gives birth to despair. It is true the dark night is a dangerous time. The devil will be working overtime to play on our vanity and self-pity. Sometimes, unfortunately, he will succeed. But if we hang on blindly in the face of his onslaughts, we will find that the Lord is far stronger than Satan, and that the humility, docility, and love which he is implanting in us, precisely by means of darkness, will make despair a more and more impossible option for us.

Thus it is that I have said that the soul living in authentic darkness is really infinitely far from despair. Its darkest moments will be just before the dawn, and when the dawn suddenly breaks upon the heart that has been desiring it with its whole being, the whole long night which has passed will seem a small enough price to pay for the wondrous joy of the new day.

There is another striking feature of the resurrection narratives which is equally important to the one who prays. We have been speaking of the Easter experience which seems to herald the end of the long dark night of the soul. And yet we said earlier that this darkness will normally be the lifetime experience of the mature prayer. Is there not a contradiction, or at least a paradox, here? Paradox, yes; contradiction, no. If we look back at the events of the first Easter day, we notice a common pattern to all of the Lord's appearances. Once he had convinced the disciples that it was really he, once their doubts had been transformed into that beautiful "disbelief for sheer joy," he quickly disappeared from their sight.

By a happy coincidence, I am writing these lines on the feast of Mary Magdalene, the very first witness to the Lord's resurrection. In the gospel reading for her feast (Jn 20:1–18), we find the pattern of all subsequent resurrection experiences, in the apostles' lives and in our own. When at last she recognized him, Magdalene could not contain her joy. She must have thrown herself at his feet—this woman from whom he had driven seven devils, who could not imagine a life without him now—and clung to his ankles. She had lost him once and now she would never let him go again! But Jesus had other ideas. The meaning of the resurrection, once Mary truly grasped it, was that she no longer had to cling to him out of fear of losing him. If he is truly risen as he said, then he is Lord. Death and darkness have been conquered, and we need never fear losing him again.

Here is the last, and perhaps the greatest, inversion of all natural ways of seeing. To truly possess the Lord is to be so secure in his love that we need not cling to him ever again. The experience of the resurrection means that we need never again fear the darkness or even death. "'Death is swallowed up in victory. O death, where is your victory? O death, where is your sting?' The sting of death is sin, and sin gets its power from the law" (1 Cor 15:54–56). Paul is speaking here of the last day, when our corruptible frame takes on incorruptibility. Only then will we possess fully the fruits, the security of our resurrection faith. Long before that, for those who have experienced the purgatory of the dark night, there comes a peace—rooted not in ourselves, who always "carry our treasure in fragile vessels," but in the Lord who has loved us unto death and has risen in glory for us—a peace which the world cannot take away. Paul reflects this in the verse which immediately follows his triumphant interrogation of death: "But thanks be to God who has given us the victory through our Lord Jesus Christ." "Has given"—the victory is already won!

Only if we forget what he has been for us could we ever lose our Easter peace. This certainty and security, however, is not for ourselves alone. It is not a treasure to be hoarded and gloated over. That would be to cling to the Lord. Instead, we must, like Magdalene and the Emmaus disciples, return to the brethren, to the persons and places of our ordinary lives, to share the good news that the Lord is risen. The gift of the resurrection is never a gift to be hoarded to our bosoms like a miser's money (the image which St. Paul probably has in mind in describing Jesus' self-emptying in Philippians 2:6: "He did not deem equality with God something to be grasped at"); it is a gift which we can only keep by giving it away. Jesus was "greatly exalted" by the Father precisely because he "emptied himself" (Phil 2:5–11). It must be the same with Magdalene, with the disciples, with us. The test of the genuineness of our experience of the risen Lord is precisely our need, even at the cost of not clinging to him, to share the good news with those who have not yet seen him.

This is true of all genuine prayer, as we have seen in chapter 2. The water is for the flowers; prayer is for the virtues, and a crucial virtue in the garden of the Lord is our zeal for the spread of his kingdom and the glorification of his name. What we are saying now, in discussing the situation of those who have lived through the dark night and seen the first flush of the dawn of the resurrection, is that this need to share, to "freely give what we have freely received," becomes even more urgent and compelling. When we arrive at the "high places" in the company of Sorrow and Suffering, we find ourselves, like Much-Afraid, impelled to return to the Valley of Humiliation to share with our "Fearing" relatives all we have discovered.[7] Our zeal now, however, is quite different from the earlier stages of our prayer life. In the first place it is much purer, more "God centered," because of the purifying darkness through which we have been living. Perhaps without our realizing it, the living flame of love has been burning out of us all the vanity and self-seeking which mar even our most generous human acts. If we have persevered in prayer even without the reward of consolation, even when prayer seemed to offer us not bliss but misery, it is a clear sign that something very important has been happening to our hierarchy of values. We have learned to seek "the God of consolations and not the consolations of God." We have moved, imperceptibly, from loving (for the fulfillment it gives us) to truly loving (simply because God is God). And such a tremendous change in our prayer cannot but effect a comparable change in our lives. Our apostolate, our ministry, our service of others also becomes more other-centered and less self-centered. We begin to realize how all our generous and apostolic actions have been tainted by seeking for recognition, by a need to prove our own worth, and perhaps our superiority to others (how hard it is to say and really mean with Paul that "I did the planting, Apollos did the watering, but God gave growth. In this, neither the planter nor the waterer counts for anything, only God, who gives growth"(1 Cor 3:6–7); by a desire to find our fulfillment in others' dependence on us. The very fire which illumines our own darkness also gradually burns out of us all of these impurities, in our prayer and in our work for the Lord.

• • •

The Real Meaning of the "False Dawn"

I realize now that this is the reason why my own experience at the Naga Carmel—a genuine resurrection experience—left me with the strong sense that I was much more secure in the dark. I saw then that there was much self-seeking in my prayer, and I think I had long realized that there was much vanity in my work for others. It was a constant and exasperating refrain in my daily examination of conscience! What I realize now is that the darkness of prayer was the way—the only way, since my own efforts seemed to effect very little change—in which this "rapine in the holocaust" would gradually be removed. As I look back over the years now, I can see the healing which the darkness has already effected in me, and I thank the Lord for it. But I can also guess (may you find things different in yourself!) that much darkness still lies ahead, because this weed of vanity seems to have incredibly deep roots. The difference between now and the pre-Naga days is that I can now bless the darkness and desire that the Lord continue with his healing surgery. Only when it is accomplished will my work, and not only my prayer, be wholly for him as it should be.

We have implied that we can only realize what the dark night is working in us when the darkness lifts and the dawn returns. When the darkness is deep we will have very little sense that anything good is happening. But from time to time the Lord will lift the veil. He will remove the log from the fire, and then it will be possible to see and to rejoice in what is being done in the searing darkness of contemplation. It is then that I will be able to see in myself the growing humility, fraternal love, obedience of which John speaks and this will be a source of great joy, particularly because it will be clear that this growth is not at all due to my own efforts but has happened, as it were, while I slept, while nothing at all seemed to be happening.[8]

These times of tranquility may seem to mark the end of our purification, a definitive emergence "out of the darkness into his wonderful light" (1 Pt 2:9). But, as the foregoing lines suggest, what we experience is really more of a false dawn—a premature foretaste of what will be when God has truly become the all-encompassing Light of our souls. Yet, the false dawn is, in itself, quite true. What we see is real and the light by which we see is truly the Lord. The falseness comes from our expectations: We hunger for the real dawn, and in our eagerness we say, "This is it!" When it turns out to be but the first rosy finger of what is still to come, our expectations are frustrated and disappointed. This simply means (if we may be allowed to mix our metaphors) that we have not really learned yet to float free in the sea of the Lord.

When we are able to accept the humbling fact that this is so (usually because the darkness returns again), we begin to see the real meaning of the light of the false dawn. While our growth in humility, fraternal love, obedience is not all that we expect or would like, it is very real. There is another change which we discover in ourselves which is equally real and equally wonderful, a change which makes our understanding of our mission in the world quite different. We begin to discover that in floating free we are going somewhere, somewhere we cannot predict or control, but a place far better than the destination and the route we have charted for ourselves. The only way I can express the experience is to say that we become spectators at the unfolding of our own lives. We realize that, not only in prayer but in external events, we are not the ones writing the script of

173

our lives. What happens to us becomes a matter of wonder even to ourselves! We begin to discover, to discern (for this is the deepest meaning of discernment) the shape of the vessel which the potter is fashioning.

Since our lives are inevitably interwoven with the lives of those we love and serve, this discovery gradually extends to the whole of our world. We begin to realize that the more we are totally surrendered to the Lord's will in us (and this, as we have seen, is the whole purpose and fruit of the dark night), the more wondrous are the works we see him do through us in others. Compare this discussion of the advantages of the dark night with what Boase has to say.[9] As he notes, we now begin to discover what it means to pray always. When praying meant "thinking" for us, we could scarcely be apostles and pray-ers (i.e., think of two distinct things) at one and the same time. But now that our prayer has moved to a much deeper level of our being, we realize, albeit obscurely, that it is indeed possible to pray even in the midst of intense apostolic involvement. In this sense all our service becomes prayer, and all our work play!

As I mentioned in chapter 1, I am the son of a man who wore both a belt and suspenders. True to my heritage and perhaps my genes, I, too, am a planner, an organizer, not one to leave things to chance. That is the reason, perhaps, why the experience of letting go, and of being happy to let go, seems so extraordinary and grace-filled to me. Sometimes I ask, "Is this really me?" and then some touch of the old belt-and-suspender mentality surfaces to assure me it really is!

Since I am also the spiritual son of a man, Ignatius Loyola, who must rank as one of the most active and organized of the saints—it is not surprising that I find myself a take-charge sort of person. It is in my genes, both biological and spiritual! But that just makes all the more remarkable the change that I have seen in myself over the years, as I discover that I do float, I do listen; I am a spectator at my own life's unfolding, far more than I would ever have imagined possible. Best of all, I find I like and value the experience! It is very hard to explain to those who "have promises to keep, and miles to go before (they) sleep," especially to those seized by a divine restlessness to do great things for God. But somehow I feel sure it is the right way for me—the way of the clay in the potter's hands.

Moreover, I am becoming convinced that it is really the only way. This is a dangerous claim to make in this activist age in which we live, when the church is in ferment with a great desire to change structures, to change persons, to provide an ideology and a praxis for the active reform of every ill. This ferment is clearly one of the signs of the times which we must observe and reflect upon in seeking to discern the way the Spirit is working in the church. To ignore it would certainly be the height of unconcern. Yet, that very fact raises the crucial question: what form should our concern take? Is our activist spirit a contemporary and very subtle way of manipulating God? Or is it a discerning response to the word of the Lord being spoken in our midst? Does our activism come from our own ideas of what should be, which we then conclude are—have to be—the Lord's ideas, too, or does it come from the Spirit stirring the waters among us?[10] For years I myself resisted this letting go of everything into the hands of God. It seemed too passive, too fatalistic—particularly for a Jesuit committed to a continual quest for the "greater glory of God." Did that not mean to do great things myself? That is what I wanted it to mean, but the Lord had other ideas! And so, with all due respect for the convictions of those who discern differently, I can only say now that the Lord seems to tell me that "the way of the clay" is the only Christian way, that the command to "turn the other cheek" (Lk 6:29; Mt 5:29) is not a culturally conditioned command which the Lord would revise if he

175

lived today, but a permanent part of the life, the prayer, and the work, of the follower of Christ.

• • •

Why Floating Is the Only Way

Why the only way? Because, as I read the gospels, it seems clearly the way of Jesus, who asserts emphatically: "By himself the Son can do nothing; he can only do what he sees the Father doing: and whatever the Father does, the Son does too" (Jn 5:19). In the discourse on the bread of life, when the crowd asks him to "give us that bread always," he replies: "Everyone whom the Father gives me will come to me; I will certainly not reject anyone who comes to me, because I have come from heaven, not to do my own will, but to do the will of him who sent me" (Jn 6:37–38). His disciples are given him by the Father (6:44, 65), as is his doctrine (7:16; 8:40); it is the Father who attests to the authenticity of his mission (8:18). Even his glory, his vindication, is not his own proper concern but the Father's: "I do not seek my own glory; there is someone who does seek it and is the judge of it" (8:50; see 8:54). The picture, which could be confirmed by numerous other statements of Jesus himself in the gospels, is of a man totally given to the Father's will, a man who—by the mysterious union of the divine with the human in him which we call the hypostatic union—has discovered fully the lesson of the dark night.

For us the process is much more painful, since he was like us in every way "except only sin" (Heb 4:15), and it is the sinfulness in us which makes the process of divinization slow and difficult. But the goal is the same: to abide in him, to keep his commandments, to be his friends "because I have made known to you everything I have learnt from my Father" (Jn 15:15). It is this total identification which the dark cloud of unknowing is effecting in us—an identification which is not only interior and mystical but which extends to the most active moments of our lives. "The life I live now is not my own; Christ is living in me" (Gal 2:20). The older translation, which is more literal in rendering the Greek original, is even more powerful: "I live, no longer I, but Christ lives in me." Paul is talking here not merely of his interior life but of his ministry, his doctrine, his mission.

We see the same thing in St. Ignatius, that restless caballero for Christ, who spent the last fifteen years of his life chained to a desk in Rome. It must have seemed like a real prison to him: all his dreams of conquering the world for Christ were to be realized only vicariously, through Francis Xavier in the Far East, through Peter Fabre and James Laynez and through thousands of his sons down the centuries. This was not the crusade Ignatius had envisioned for himself, but it was what "pleased the Father." We can safely guess that a real dark night was involved as Ignatius came to see things the Lord's way. Ignatius (and Ignatius' ideas of what would glorify God) had to die so that Christ might truly be born in him. He wrote his *Spiritual Exercises* in the early years of his conversion as a means "to help the retreatant to conquer himself, and to regulate his life so that he will not be influenced in his decisions by any inordinate attachment."[11] At first he must have been thinking of the attachments to our honor, our families, our material possessions (the type of inordinate desires which John of the Cross discusses in Book I of the *Ascent of Mount Carmel*, which are the object of the active purification of the soul). But there are deeper attachments, more subtle and harder to root out, which we begin to discover only when we are already committed to the Lord: the attachment to my own ideas of how God should be working in me and through me, the deeper vanity which is disguised as zeal. These are the inordinate desires which the active purification alone (our own ascetical efforts) cannot root out; John discusses them in the first

177

seven chapters of the *Dark Night of the Soul,* because only the dark night, the experience of the dry well which has been the subject of this book, can burn them out of us.

When there are hints of the dawn in this dark night—even of that false dawn which heralds the true—we discover that the dry darkness is indeed doing its work. It is painfully slow, and we feel perhaps that we are drifting farther away from Jesus' own "passion for God." But we are not; we are actually closer to our goal, but much more aware of the immense distance to be traversed. This would be discouraging except for one beautiful realization: Even the distance and the traversing of the distance are the Lord's responsibility! We cannot worry about it because it is not ours to remedy. Everything, literally everything, is in his hands.

• • •

The Floater and Her Brethren

When we realize this—realize it experientially—we have truly learned to float. Deep down we know, and are happy in the knowledge, that the life of floating which has begun will last for eternity. Floaters in the sea of God never swim again—nor do they have any desire to. The wonders of floating fill their every desire. If only those around them, the brethren they love—some swimming strenuously, some clinging to rafts of their own making, some building huts to settle on the shore—could realize that floating is the only answer! But that is the Lord's concern; what he has done for the floaters he will surely do for the others, if only they let him. Since he waited so long for us, he will surely wait for them. In the meantime our floating may be a sign, a sacrament, of what can be. After all, it was just such a sign, from others floating ahead of us, which first drew us to the water!

When we begin to realize that the darkness is light, and that ever so slowly the Lord of love is fashioning in us the eyes to see, the dominant motif of our prayer becomes gratitude—gratitude even, and perhaps especially, for the trials which have previously caused us misery, since we now realize that it is precisely through these trials that the Lord is fashioning in us the resurrection person. And our greatest joy, our greatest expression of gratitude, is to be able to share with others the good news which we have learned: "We are writing this to you so that our joy may be complete!" (1 Jn 1:4).

EPILOGUE:

BLESSED ARE
THE POOR IN SPIRIT

• • •

As we come to the end of our exploration of that critical stage of the soul's journey to God which is the move from knowing to loving to truly loving, I ask myself: What one phrase or image can capture the whole reality which I have been trying, so inadequately, to describe in human words? Perhaps no single phrase or image can ever bear such a burden of meaning. But there are two, the first a gospel phrase and the second an image from my own experience, which for me come close to capturing what the mature life of prayer is all about. The image might easily be the dark night, the cloud of unknowing, the dry well in the flowering garden; but for me it is none of these. Rather, it is the image of floating, which formed the leitmotif of chapter 6 and which, like the potter's clay, has continued to reveal new meaning to me as the years have passed.

The gospel phrase is much less original or idiosyncratic. It is, in fact, the first of the beatitudes: "How blest are the poor in spirit: the kingdom of Heaven is theirs" (Mt 5:3).

Jesus began the Sermon on the Mount with this blessing. It is one we are familiar with from childhood and, on the face of it, the meaning seems abundantly clear. Yet, for some years I have puzzled over its real meaning.

• • •

Who Are the Poor in Spirit?

The poor are the anawim, the dispossessed of Israel, those whose wealth is not material but the love of the Lord. But material poverty is not the ideal Jesus is proposing. This seems clear from the contrast he himself draws between the lifestyle of John the Baptist and his own: "John came, neither eating nor drinking, and they say, 'He is possessed!' The Son of man came, eating and drinking, and they say, 'Look, a glutton and a drunkard, a friend of tax collectors and sinners'" (Mt 11:18–19). His way of life must have appeared quite ordinary, even bourgeois, to his opponents. It is true that he asked some—Peter and John and James and the rich young man—to leave everything in order to follow him. But there were others whom he loved, and whose company he shared—Mary and Martha and Lazarus, Simon, Zacchaeus—of whom he seems to have made no comparable demand.[1] Moreover, his reaction to the criticism of the woman who anointed his head with costly ointment, which by implication was a criticism of himself for allowing her to do it,[2] is scarcely the reaction of one for whom material poverty is of the very essence of the kingdom. The objection was that the jar of perfume might have been sold for 300 silver pieces (ten times the amount for which Judas was to sell Jesus!) "and the money given to the poor." Jesus replies, "Why are you upsetting the woman? What she has done for me is indeed a good work. You have the poor with you always, but you will not always have me. . . . In truth I tell you, wherever the good news is proclaimed, what she has done will be told as well, in remembrance of her" (Mt 26:10–11, 13).

His attitude toward material possessions is really paradoxical. He certainly possessed very little, especially considering what he might have chosen for himself as the incarnate Son of God. Yet, he does not seem to have placed much importance on this material dispossession in itself. It was John the Baptist who came "neither eating nor drinking," whose life symbolized a radical stripping off of the goods of this world. Jesus, by contrast, promised not only eternal life but also "a hundred times as much, houses, brothers, sisters, mothers, children, and land" to all those who left everything for his sake and the sake of the gospel (Mk 10:29–30).

Thus, the paradox which puzzled me for many years: Given these promises, and given the contrast which Jesus draws between himself and John, what is the poverty of spirit which claims first place in the beatitudes and whose reward is the kingdom of heaven? The surface answer is clear enough. Somehow the ideal Jesus is proposing, the demand he is making, is what we have come to call "detachment." It is not what we possess but what we are attached to—what possesses us—which makes us unfit for, incapable of inheriting the kingdom of God. This need for detachment is present from the very beginning of the interior life; that is why the active purification of the soul is a crucial element in laying a solid spiritual foundation.

This much was clear enough to me long ago—very difficult to live but clear enough in principle. Moreover, I could see quite well that actual material poverty, while not of the essence of the beatitude, could be a great help, both personally and apostolically, to its realization. Personally, because our possessions (persons as well as things) are the roots from which spring the vines of attachment which entangle our hearts. And apostolically, since we can scarcely preach detachment effectively unless it is concretely symbolized in the way we live. We may indeed possess much and yet be truly free, detached inwardly (poor in spirit), but it is hard to see how flesh-and-blood people could really hear and be convinced by our witness to the need for detachment unless it is concretely embodied in our way of life, in our own flesh and blood. What we are speaks much louder than what we say, and what we are can only be revealed to others by the way we live.

As I said above, this surface answer to our question about the meaning of poverty of spirit is clear enough. Difficult indeed to live, but clear enough in principle. Still, the beatitude has puzzled me for many years. I felt there must be something more there, something deeper than what I had seen. It was only when I made that thirty-day retreat in Antique in 1977 that the "something more" seemed to be revealed to me. Quite unexpectedly, the idea of poverty of spirit became the theme of the whole thirty days. Gradually I began to see what it really meant for me, and how it was connected with the long experience of the dry well which this book (and, if I am not mistaken, a substantial part of the interior life) is all about.

• • •

Why Floaters Are (and Become) the Poor in Spirit

The insight, like most of the turning-point insights of my life, can be put very simply: Poverty of spirit means to have no will of my own. At root it is not surrendering things, or my attachment to things, but surrendering my very will. As long as we can choose the things, the attachments, to surrender—even if we choose to surrender all of them—it is still we who are choosing; it is still our will which is in control. As long as it is we who are stripping ourselves, we are

183

not truly poor in spirit. The beatitude which Jesus proclaims is only realized—made real—in us when we have let go of our own will, even our will to become holy!

This, as I say, was the insight which dominated my own thirty-day retreat in Antique. Perhaps it was no accident that another striking experience was also quite common during that same period of my life: very often, when I was most at peace, I seemed to see my own life as a movie—a movie of which I was not the producer or director. I found myself a spectator even at the unfolding of my own destiny! It was a very strange experience, particularly for someone so temperamentally an activist as myself. Even though, with time, I have become more at home with the sensation, it is still a strange feeling. It is not natural to be a floater. Even when we do learn a bit about floating and acquire some skill at it, there still lurks in us a suspicion that we should be doing something, controlling events, working for the kingdom according to our own lights and our own God-given natural gifts. So we should, as long as we are guided by the light of our own God-given reason. Reason alone, even guided by grace, will never make us floaters. What we do under grace to dispose ourselves for God and to respond to God can never bring us to float. John of the Cross's "active purification," the subject of the *Ascent of Mount Carmel,* can bring us to the water and lead us to swim toward God, but it is only the passive purification, what God does in us when he takes over wholly the work of our transformation, which can make floaters out of swimmers.

Floaters are not drifters. To the outside observer they appear very much alike—both passive in the face of events. But I have learned from experience that floating is far more dynamic and responsive than it appears. If I just drift in the water, my legs inevitably tend to settle towards the bottom and soon my balance is lost. The drifters are not responsive to the current and the waves; they have a will of their own—the will to be lazy—and are soon upended by the tide.

The floaters, by contrast, have allowed the will of the water to become their own. They have no will of their own, and yet they are intensely active. The will of the water, the will of the sea which is God, has become the dynamic force of their lives and all their energies are spent in responding fully to the ebb and flow of the tide. They are intensely active. What is lacking in their life is tension, the tension which the swimmers experience between their own efforts and the contrary pull of the water. The swimmers have two wills pulling them, their own and God's, and this is what makes swimming exhausting. For the "sinner" who has not yet realized and accepted that God is the goal of his life, the tension can tear him apart. But even those who have found God as the goal of their lives will still experience another kind of tension, the tension which Paul describes so unforgettably in Romans 7. The tension lasts as long as they seek to swim toward their goal, that is, as long as they seek to control the journey. Even though they and God have the same goal (the salvation and sanctification of themselves and of their world), they will still be in tension concerning the means. It is only the floaters, who have allowed the will of the Lord to become their own will, who will be intensely active and yet tension-free.

Peace, as Augustine has said, is not the absence of activity or effort but the tranquility of order. Where there is order there is peace, even in the midst of strenuous activity. Where there is one will—God's will—there is order. It is only where there are two wills—God's and mine—that tension and disorder prevail.

We have, then, a paradox: To have no will of my own, to be truly poor in spirit, is not really to have no will but to have only one will. That is why the poor in spirit are not spineless, wishy-washy souls devoid of energy and initiative. They are, in fact, the real doers in the kingdom of God, precisely because they are totally and passionately surrendered to the will of God. Having no will of their own, all their energies can be harnessed to the work of God in the world; all their loves and talents, and limitations, too, can be animated totally by his will.

I said earlier that this insight into the meaning of poverty of spirit was the dominant theme of my thirty-day retreat in 1977. There is, of course, a great difference between realizing what poverty of spirit is and actually living it. I am still very far from the latter, but that distance between ideal and reality is an indication of the whole point of this book. We cannot become truly poor in spirit in this deeper sense by virtue of any efforts of our own. It is only the dry well, the dark night, the cloud of unknowing which can effect this radical purification in us. Only the Lord can make us truly poor in spirit and thus rightful heirs of the kingdom of God. That, in fact, is precisely what he is doing in the process we have described in Part Two above. The long walk in darkness, with occasional, unpredictable, uncontrollable periods of light, is his way of emptying us of our own will so that we may be possessed by his will and thus made divine (see Mt 5:48; Gal 2:20). Boase, who calls this passive purification the "prayer of faith," expresses beautifully the goal of it all:

> The Prayer of Faith, with its long drilling in emptiness and desolation, leads us slowly but surely to a state in which it is all one to us whether we are in sunlight or in cloud, provided only that on our part there is complete, unreserved, uncalculating, unrestricted yielding of our whole being into God's hands. It is this which is the neverceasing activity which underlies even the apparently most paralytic inactivity in the desolations of this prayer.[3]

The Role of Our Active Lives
in Making Us Floaters

For those of us who are called to live an active life "in the world," it is important to note that God works this transforming purification not only in the darkness of prayer but in all the ups and downs, the trials of our active life.[4] This, at least, is the conviction I have come to after years of reflecting on the teaching of great contemplatives like St. John of the Cross. They focus on the inner purifying darkness of formal prayer, and for this reason their teaching can seem somewhat unrealistic for people called to live an active, apostolic life. But I am convinced it is not at all unrealistic, once we begin to see God working his purification equally in the darkness of prayer and in the frustrations of our life of service. Both are part of the same passive purification for us apostles and laity; in fact, I believe it is part of our vocation that the inner darkness of prayer will most often have its roots in the external hardships of a life of service: the disappointments, misunderstandings, failures, "bad days" which are an inevitable part of raising a family or living in a community or proclaiming the gospel. Talk about contemplation, formal prayer, dark nights seems unreal to us only because we fail to realize that God works in all the events of our life, interior and exterior. For those who have begun to be contemplatives in action, everything is part of that passive purification of which we have been speaking.[5]

Can I illustrate this more concretely? When I look at my own life, it is the accidents which reveal most clearly the hand of God at work purifying me of my own will. I think I first became aware of this in an apparently trivial series of incidents. As I have said, I am naturally a planner, an organizer, a "take charge" sort of person. In my earlier years in the seminary, I often had elaborate plans for holiday outings and seminary activities. Sometimes these plans were realized and sometimes not. Gradually I began to realize that the best planned outings, where everything went as anticipated, left me somehow empty afterward. By contrast, unplanned surprises—contrary to my temperament and my expectations—often left the happiest memories. The more I had anticipated the results in detail, the less satisfying the outcome proved to be. Even with friendships, the more consciously I cultivated them and sought to shape them to my expectations, the less likely they were to be deep and lasting. Now, twenty-five years later, I am ashamed to say that my most lasting friendships are the ones I once most took for granted.

In themselves, these incidents might seem merely in- dications of my own peculiar psychological makeup. But I have learned that the Lord was really at work even then. The subsequent pattern has confirmed this: I came to the Philippines "by accident," after spending three years pre- paring myself for Japan! I came to San Jose Seminary "by ac- cident," when the man who was preferred for the job proved to be unavailable. So it has gone since, to the extent that the accidental has more and more come to seem normal. It is not that I don't plan. I do, since that seems a necessary part of my cooperation with the Lord; but I find I have learned to "hang loose" about the fulfillment of my plans—and to expect surprises as the best parts of the drama, despite the uncertainty and darkness, and even desolation, they entail. Somehow—and this is the point of burdening the reader with these personal details—my external life and my inner life are all one. The Lord is working in all areas to bring me—and, I am convinced, everyone who prays sincerely— to a genuine poverty of spirit. The inner and the outer are not in conflict once we realize this. In both areas the well runs dry, and by means of this passive purification the Lord accomplishes in us what Teilhard has called the "diviniza- tion of our passivities."

The River Flows Back to Eternity

Once we realize what is happening, it makes more sense to say that the dark night, the dry well, will be the experience of most faithful prayers most of their lives. In fact, we never return to the light we knew before; we never do go to the well again for the water we seek. That light proves to be no light, and that water no water, once we pass the point of no return. When and how we will pass this point, though, must be left to the Lord. Even here, at this deepest level of our desire for God, we must have "no will of our own." When this is true of us, the kingdom of God will be ours, for we will be truly poor in spirit. Then the dry well will seem a small price, indeed, to pay: "Whoever drinks this water will be thirsty again; no one who drinks the water that I shall give will ever be thirsty again; the water that I shall give will become a spring of water within, welling up for eternal life" (Jn 4:13–14).

As I wrote in my journal at the end of that Antique retreat in 1977:

> My Lord, my Love,
> You have called me
> To float blind down the dark river which leads to
> the kingdom of light.
> May my journey be for the healing
> Of those to whom you send me
> Who walk in the shadow of death.

What remains for the floater is the wondrous discovery that the river on which he floats springs, as John says, from the very heart of God.

> Then the angel showed me the river of life rising from the throne of God and of the Lamb and flowing crystal clear. Down the middle of the city

street, on either bank of the river, were the trees of life, which bear twelve crops of fruit in a year, one in each month, and the leaves of which are the cure for the nations (Rev 22:1–2).

Now the tide is reversed and the river draws the floater back to its Source. But who can describe, or even imagine, what the floater will discover there?

NOTES

Foreword

1. Sandra M. Schneiders, "Contemporary Religious Life: Death or Transformation," *Cross Currents*, 46 (4), Winter 1996/97, 510–535.

Preface

1. The Oblates of Notre Dame are a Filipino congregation of sisters founded by Fr. George Dion, O.M.I.; they work in partnership with the Oblate Fathers in the Muslim areas of the country.

Introduction

1. Ave Maria Press, Notre Dame, Indiana, 1977 (also St. Paul Press, Manila, Philippines, 1977).
2. "Contemplation" is used here in the active, acquired, Ignatian sense which was explained in chapter 6 of *Opening to God*. The Carmelite (Teresa's and John's) sense of contemplation as a passive, infused way of praying is really the central topic of this new book.
3. This passage is discussed in chapter 4.
4. Leonard Boase, S.J., *Prayer of Faith*, originally published by the Apostleship of Prayer, Wimbledon, England, 1950. The book was reissued in a rearranged,

popularized (and, in my judgment, less helpful) form published by Our Sunday Visitor (Huntington, Indiana) and Darton, Longman, Todd (London, England) in 1976. Boase's original work was reprinted by Loyola University Press of Chicago in 1985. I was able to express my gratitude to him by writing the foreword to that edition.

5. This comparison might not seem very felicitous, save to those who delight in Wodehouse as much as I do. Wodehouse has been put down as "the performing flea" of English literature, but there seem to be many who feel as I do, that it is a serious achievement to puncture our pompous balloons and to help us to take ourselves less seriously. Teresa would have liked the Cloud—and Wodehouse, too. One of her sagest pieces of advice is to take God very seriously, but not to take ourselves seriously at all!

6. *Living Flame of Love*, Stanza 3, #28–58 (#29–67 in the Second Redaction).

7. Letter to Doña Juana de Pedraza, January 28, 1589. Included in *The Collected Works of St. John of the Cross* (translated by Kieran Kavanaugh, O.C.D. and Otilio Rodriguez, O.C.D.), Washington, DC: ICS Publications, 1973, pp. 690–691.

8. There will always be more to know, of course, both with human lovers and with God. In fact, since God is infinite and inexhaustible goodness, we will, throughout eternity, always be just beginning to discover who he is for us. But here I side with Bonaventure and the Franciscans, with their emphasis on the will and on love, as contrasted with Thomas and the Dominicans, who lay relatively greater stress on the intellect and on knowledge: it is not this knowledge, even of the Lord, which is the core of the mature pray-er's experience.

More and more, knowledge becomes the handmaiden of love, the intellect the handmaid of the heart. We begin to realize clearly (as we stressed even in *Opening to God*) that praying is essentially not knowing but loving the Lord—that the "knowing" of John 17:3, which is equated with eternal life, is essentially Pascal's knowledge of the heart.

9. St. John of the Cross has a classic discussion of this point in chapters 35 to 45 of Book III of the *Ascent of Mount Carmel*. He speaks there of statues, beautiful churches, religious ceremonies, inspiring sermons. They are all means to devotion and can help beginners to experience God; but, according to John, the time will come when our attachment to these means becomes an obstacle to a deeper encounter with the Lord. We should use them as long as they help us to God, but we should also be able to abandon them if and when they become a hindrance to the Lord's deeper gift of himself to us.

10. In later years I came to feel the same affection for *Darkness in the Marketplace* (Ave Maria Press, 1991) and *Prayer and Common Sense* (Ave Maria Press, 1995)—and for the same reason!

11. Antoine de Saint Exupery, *The Little Prince* (New York: Harbrace Paperbound, 1971, pp. 87–88).

CHAPTER 1

• • •

1. See, for example, Psalms 1 and 23; Isaiah 32:2; 43:19-20; Jeremiah 2:13; 17:13. For an excellent summary discussion of the biblical importance of water, see John McKenzie's *Dictionary of the Bible* (Bruce, 1965), under the entry "water."

2. For example, the number 12 plays a prominent role in John's symbolism. It is the number of the tribes of Israel, and thus symbolizes the full complement of God's people. The number 144,000 symbolizes all the people who will be brought into the eternal kingdom of God (144 being 12 times 12 and thus symbolizing absolute completeness). Some groups have misunderstood this kind of symbolic language and have come to believe, for example, that only and exactly 144,000 people will be saved.

3. Two beautiful examples are Anne Morrow Lindbergh's *Gift from the Sea* (New York: New American Library, 1955) and David Walker's *God Is a Sea* (Sydney: Alba House, 1977).

4. In *Opening to God* I compared books on prayer to cookbooks, my point being that they are not just to be read cover-to-cover, but are guides to action. We read the cookbook when we want to cook something, and we

study those pages which we actually expect to use here and now. When *Opening to God* appeared, one of my married cousins wrote to me to say how much she liked it and how she was using it in her CCD work as a religion teacher. Her only objection, she said, was that "I must admit that I read it cover to cover, but then I also read cookbooks cover-to-cover!" Many other women have since told me the same thing, which goes to prove how little a celibate really knows about the relationship between a woman and her cookbook! Actually, as I write these lines, I realize that the same problem arises with regard to maps: I am one of those queer people who love maps (the kind of person who keeps the National Geographic Society in business), and enjoy poring over them even when I am not going anywhere. So every analogy limps!

5.   The above development of the map analogy is due to my own reflection on a brief but very helpful insight of Leonard Boase, S.J., *Prayer of Faith*. In the 1985 edition, the map analogy is on p. 38.

6.   This point, that reading about prayer can never substitute for actually praying, needs to be emphasized in our day. There is, thank God, a great interest in prayer today. But there is a danger that we think we are prayerful simply because of the number of books we read or lectures we attend, and the warm glow that accompanies such activity. Thus, when I myself had to choose between giving conferences and individual direction, I felt compelled to give preference to the latter. I shared my decision with a friend, a Dominican sister, and she wrote in reply; "I think your decision is right. Today everyone wants to hear about prayer, but the time comes when we have to stop talking about it

and start praying." No number of inspiring lectures or books alone will ever make us pray.

7. *Autobiography*, St. Teresa of Avila, chapter XI, 6-7. The quotations are taken from *The Collected Works of St. Teresa of Avila*, Volume One, translated by Kieran Kavanaugh, O.C.D., and Otilio Rodriguez, O.C.D. (ICS Publications, Washington, DC, 1976). There is also a more recent translation by John Clarke, O.C.D. (ICS Publications, Washington, DC, 1996).

8. Since one of the plants in the Lord's garden is a growing awareness of our own sinfulness, it can be difficult for us to recognize growth in ourselves. That is, as we grow we may well feel we are slipping farther from God, not because we are regressing but because we are becoming more aware of who we really are. The closer we come to the light of God, the darker our own darkness appears by contrast. We shall have to discuss this painful but very valuable aspect of interior growth in chapter 5. For now, let us note that a good director is very important at this point. If he or she says we are on the right track and are growing, we should trust that judgment, even though we ourselves cannot see the growth.

9. *Spiritual Exercises*, #230–231 (p. 103 in the Image paperback).

10. In chapter XI Teresa says: "Here by 'water' I am referring to tears and when there are no tears to interior tenderness and feelings of devotion" (Kavanaugh and Rodriguez, p. 82). This will be important later when we discuss what is happening when the well runs dry.

11. Teresa, *Autobiography*, chapter XI (Kavanaugh and Rodriguez, pp. 80–81).

12. See Teresa's preface to the *Autobiography*.

13. Teresa, *Autobiography*, chapter XI (Kavanaugh and Rodriguez, p. 81).

14. Teresa, *Autobiography*, chapter XI (Kavanaugh and Rodriguez, p. 81).

15. Teresa, *Autobiography*, chapter XIV (Kavanaugh and Rodriguez, p. 97).

16. Teresa, *Autobiography*, chapter XIV (Kavanaugh and Rodriguez, p. 97).

17. The reference to the faculties being lost or sleeping will be clearer when we contrast this way with the third and fourth ways of drawing water, where they do "sleep" (*Autobiography*, chapter XVI), or are even "dead" (chapter XVIII).

18. Teresa, *Autobiography*, chapter XIV (Kavanaugh and Rodriguez, p. 97).

19. Teresa, *Autobiography*, chapter XIV (Kavanaugh and Rodriguez, pp. 97–98).

20. The comparison I use here was first suggested to me by Boase's metaphor of children playing in the garden of a country house. See *Prayer of Faith*, chapter IX, p. 59 of the original 1950 edition, p. 51 of the 1985 edition.

21. Teresa, *Autobiography*, chapter XIV (Kavanaugh and Rodriguez, p. 97).

22. Teresa says of the third way: "It is now, I believe, some five, or perhaps six years, since the Lord granted me this prayer in abundance," *Autobiography*, chapter XVI (translated by E. Allison Peers, Doubleday, Image Books, first published 1960). She wrote this in 1565, when she was fifty, and some twenty–nine years after her entrance into the Carmelites in 1536.

23. Teresa, *Autobiography*, chapter XVI. Teresa insists on this "instrumental" role of prayer at every stage of the interior life, and in chapter 2 we shall discuss it more fully.

24. Teresa, *Autobiography*, chapter XVI (Peers, p. 163).

CHAPTER 2

• • •

1. I believe that even Thomas Merton passed through a stage—the stage of Seeds of Contemplation (see chapter 6, "Solitude")—that would be characterized as anti-world in this sense.

2. This is mistaken, I believe, because it does not seem to harmonize with the total gospel picture of Jesus, the son of a carpenter, the friend of Lazarus, at home in the house of Simon. Jesus' point seems to be, rather, that he is too totally committed to the Father's will to be able to take root anywhere and call any place his own. He is totally "God's man," who does always the things that please the Father.

3. Ironically, the competing ideology, capitalist imperialism, also found its theoretical justification in social Darwinism. It is simply a question of which class we consider "fittest," and what ultimate "heaven" we place our faith in. The Kitchen Debate between Nixon and Khrushchev seems to exemplify perfectly the common social Darwinist ground for the first world/second world competition in our century.

4. 2 Tim 2:13. The fidelity of God as the basis of our hope is a favorite theme of St. Paul. See 1 Cor 1:9; 1 Thess 5:24; 2 Tim 3:3.

5. St. John of the Cross distinguishes two nights of the interior life: the night of the senses and the night of the soul. Despite the rather frightening name he gives to it, the dark night of the senses is really the beginning of the life of contemplative prayer. John says of it: "The night of sense is common and comes to many: These are the beginners." And later: "With regard to this way of purgation of the senses, since it is so common, we might here adduce a great number of quotations from Divine Scripture. . . . However, I do not wish to spend time upon these, for he who knows not how to look for them there will find the common experience of this purgation to be sufficient." (*Dark Night of the Soul*, Book 1, Chapter VIII, pp. 61, 63 in the 1959 Image Books translation by E. Allison Peers.) John's poetic, dramatic language may well have prevented many from recognizing the experience he describes as similar to their own. But my experience as a director confirms John's judgment that the beginning of contemplative prayer "is common and comes to many" who are faithful to prayer. It is, of course, God's pure gift and he owes it to no one, but it seems that he does will to give it freely to those who pray perseveringly. The problem is that so few people are really that serious about coming to know him!

6. The conviction that this call is equally a part of the lay vocation, especially after Vatican II, eventually led me to write *Come Down Zacchaeus* (Ave Maria Press, 1988).

7. See *Interior Castle*, "Fourth Mansions," chapter I (p. 72 in the 1961 Image Books translation by E. Allison Peers).

8. Ibid. Teresa says essentially the same thing in chapter XI of her *Autobiography*.

9. Recall that Paul's triumphant cry of hope in Romans 8 comes out of his anguished view of the human situation in Romans 7—a view which culminates in the desperate cry: "What a wretched man I am! Who will rescue me from this body doomed to death?" (7:24). This victory of Christian hope is snatched from the very jaws of human hopelessness.

10. I can reveal now, in revising this book, that Sister X is Sr. Stella Rosal, to whom this book is dedicated. In a beautiful sign of providence, she died the very day the first copies of *When the Well Runs Dry* reached the Philippines, July 22, 1979—the feast of Mary Magdalene.

11. This is the parable that provides the title for my book *Weeds Among the Wheat* (Ave Maria Press, 1984).

12. Tyndale House, Wheaton, Illinois, 1975. The allusion is to Habakkuk 3:19 (and Psalm 18:34): "God, my Lord, is my strength; he makes my feet swift as those of hinds and enables me to go upon the heights."

13. *Hind's Feet on High Places*, p. 11.

14. Tyndale House, 1976. In the preface, Hannah Hurnard makes a point relevant to our discussion of the natural defects of temperament which persist in us even as we come to know God. She reveals that Much-Afraid is really herself—"I was born with a fearful nature—a real slave of the Fearing Clan!" She shows us how all things—perhaps especially our own weaknesses—work together unto good for those whom God has called (Rom 8:28). She says, "I have tried to show as clearly as possible that the very characteristics and weaknesses of temperament with which we were born, which seem to us to be the greatest of all hindrances to the Christian life, are, in reality, the very things which, when surrendered to the Savior, can be

transformed into their exact opposites and can therefore produce in us the loveliest of all qualities." The process is painfully slow, as we have seen, but if this is the goal of it all, then, with Paul, we can truly "glory in our infirmities!"

15. Olive Press, London, 1970.

16. *Wayfarer in the Land*, p. 79. As this quotation would suggest, the "Wayfarer" of the title is not Hannah Hurnard but Jesus Christ.

CHAPTER 3

• • •

1. *Hind's Feet on High Places*, p. 55.
2. Teresa, *Autobiography*, chapter XI (Kavanaugh and Rodriguez, pp. 81-82).
3. Teresa, *Autobiography*, chapter XI (Kavanaugh and Rodriguez, p. 82).
4. See especially Jesus' dialogue with the Jews in chapters 5, 7, and 8. Jesus' total commitment, his passion for God, is beautifully summed up in 8:29: "He who sent me is with me, and has not left me to myself, for I always do what pleases him."
5. As those who have come to love Teresa know all too well, she is not an organized writer. In fact, she invented stream of consciousness writing long before the giants of twentieth-century literature appeared on the scene! This is a large part of her appeal, since we feel (as I have often felt) that she is right in the room talking with us, and often her "side trips" contain some of her most helpful insights. But the style does not make for a clear sense of sequence in the soul's journey to God. Thus it may well be that her remarks here are not intended so much for beginners as for those who have begun to draw water in the second way, by means of a pump.

6. When my sister, who was then thirty-four, read this, her comment was, "Have you spoken to any women under thirty-five lately?"

7. I explored this distinction between sin as malice and sin as sickness more fully in Day 3 of A Vacation with the Lord (Ave Maria Press, 1986) and Prayer and Common Sense (Ave Maria Press, 1995).

8. Spiritual Exercises, #322: Rule 9 of the Rules for Discernment for the First Week (p. 131 in the Image Books translation by Anthony Mottola). I would not equate desolation with dryness (though Ignatius does not distinguish between them), since desolation involves anxiety, turmoil, sadness, "loss of faith, loss of hope, loss of love" (cf. my book, Weeds Among the Wheat, Ave Maria Press, 1984, chapter 6). We can be at peace when the well runs dry, provided we understand what is happening. This is in fact the situation I envisioned in the sequel to the present book, Drinking from a Dry Well (Ave Maria Press, 1991). But dryness easily and often becomes desolation. We become anxious, discouraged, fearful when we do not understand the meaning of the dryness. The reasons Ignatius gives apply equally well to dryness and to desolation, as I have distinguished them.

9. Teresa, Autobiography, chapter XI (Kavanaugh and Rodriguez, p. 82).

10. Cf. Teresa, Interior Castle, II, 1, #6–8; IV 1, #7.

11. Hannah Hurnard, Wayfarer in the Land, p. 43.

CHAPTER 4

• • •

1. See, for example, chapter 3 of *Opening to God* (and the whole of *Weeds Among the Wheat*), where we discuss discernment of God's will as the meeting point of prayer and life. I believe the answer lies in the fact that the supreme exercise of our freedom is precisely to surrender ourselves freely to another in love, whether that other be God, a marriage partner, or a friend. Those, like Sartre, who believe that a person is thereby dehumanized, have never really grasped the difference between servitude and love. Cf. Jn 15:15: "I no longer call you servants but friends."

2. *Dark Night of the Soul*, Book 1, chapter VIII, #1 (p. 311 in the translation by Kavanaugh and Rodriguez). See also #4 (p. 313): "Not much time ordinarily passes after the initial stages of their spiritual life before beginners start to enter this night of the sense. And the majority of them do enter it, because it is common to see them suffer these aridities." On the difference between this dryness of the night of sense and the alternation of consolation and dryness which we have described in chapter 3, see chapter IX, #9 of the same Book I (p. 316).

3. *Dark Night of the Soul*, Book I, chapters VIII-X.

4. *Dark Night of the Soul*, Book I, chapter VIII (Kavanaugh and Rodriguez, p. 311).

5. St. Augustine, Tractates on the first letter of John: quoted in The Liturgy of the Hours, in The Office of Readings for the Friday of the Sixth Week in Ordinary Time.

6. *Dark Night of the Soul*, Book I, chapter IX, #1 (Kavanaugh and Rodriguez, p. 313).

7. *Dark Night of the Soul*, Book I, chapter IX, #8 (Kavanaugh and Rodriguez, p. 315).

8. Ibid., #9.

9. Cf. the *Dark Night of the Soul*, Book I, chapter X, #2 (Kavanaugh and Rodriguez, p. 317). See also St. John's letter to Doña Juana de Pedraza, October 12, 1589. She was apparently experiencing this dark night, and John insists that she should simply proceed in peace and trust his judgment that all was well. Nor should she seek for further confirmation from anyone else. "Should you have some problem, write to me about it" (pp. 699–700 in Kavanaugh and Rodriguez).

10. *Dark Night of the Soul*, Book I, chapter X, #4 (Kavanaugh and Rodriguez, p. 317).

11. It is this "being at home in the dark" that I discuss in *Drinking from a Dry Well* (Ave Maria Press, 1991). Part One discusses this "at homeness" in our life of formal prayer, Part Two, in our apostolic life.

CHAPTER 5

• • •

1. See, for example, *Dark Night of the Soul*, Book II, chapter VI, #6: ". . . their purgation here on earth is similar to that of purgatory. For this purgation is that which would have to be undergone there. The soul that endures it (the dark night) here on earth either does not enter purgatory, or is detained there for only a short while. It gains more in one hour here on earth by this purgation than it would in many there" (Kavanaugh and Rodriguez, pp. 339–340). See also chapter XX, #5 (Kavanaugh and Rodriguez, p. 377), and chapter VII, #7, where John compares the dark night to purgatory (Kavanaugh and Rodriguez, p. 343). See also The *Cloud of Unknowing*, chapter 69 (p. 137 in the Image Books edition by William Johnston, S.J., 1973).

2. *Dark Night of the Soul*, Book I, chapter IX, #4 (Kavanaugh and Rodriguez, p. 314). Leonard Boase, S.J., gives a classic description of the positive and negative aspects of the dark night (which he calls the "prayer of faith") in his book, *Prayer of Faith*, chapters XIII, XIV and XVI in the 1950 edition (London: Apostleship of Prayer) and 1985 edition (Chicago: Loyola University Press). I personally would value Boase's treatment very nearly as highly as that of John of the Cross himself,

particularly for those involved in the apostolic or active life.

3. *Dark Night of the Soul*, Book I, chapter VIII, #1 (Kavanaugh and Rodriguez, p. 311).

4. *Dark Night of the Soul*, Book II, chapter X, #1 (Kavanaugh and Rodriguez, p. 350). John returns to this famous image of the log becoming fire in the *Living Flame of Love*, stanza 1, #4ff., #16ff., etc. The image was already a part of the tradition of Christian prayer long before John, but it is he who develops it most beautifully and to greatest effect.

5. *Dark Night of the Soul*, Book I, chapter X, #4 (Kavanaugh and Rodriguez, p. 317).

6. *Dark Night of the Soul*, Book II, chapter VII, #3 (Kavanaugh and Rodriguez, p. 344–345).

7. The stages of this transforming work of God are the basis of John's distinction between the dark night of the senses, which serves to "accommodate sense to spirit" by removing the actual imperfections of our outer and inner (memory, understanding, imagination) senses, and the dark night of the spirit, which serves to "unite the spirit with God" by removing the habitual imperfections, i.e., "the imperfect habits and affections which have remained all the time in the spirit" even when the dark night of the senses was doing its purifying work in us. John compares the two kinds of imperfections to the branch and the root. The dark night of the senses removes the branches of sin, the visible manifestations of our sinful tendencies. But the roots are still there in the spirit and can bring forth new shoots again; it is only in the radical surgery of the dark night of the spirit that our vices are really radically uprooted. John's explanation makes clear the reason for the discouraging experience which Paul

describes in Romans 7. I have really seen the goodness of God and have given my life to him and yet the sinful tendencies of the old self still are actively at work in me, opposing what I truly have given my heart to. (*Dark Night of the Soul*, Book II, chapter XI, #1 (Kavanaugh and Rodriguez, p. 352).

8. The *Cloud of Unknowing*, Foreword, p. 44 in the Image Books rendition in modern English by William Johnston, S.J. (1973). See also chapter 74 (pp. 143–144). The seventy-five brief chapters of the Cloud (some only one-half page in length) cover just 100 pages, in the Johnston edition. Also included is *The Book of Privy Counselling* (i.e., spiritual direction), an even shorter and equally beautiful work by the same anonymous author.

9. Johnston discusses this question briefly in his Introduction to the Image edition of the Cloud (pp. 30–31), and in his notes to the text (pp. 189ff.) he gives numerous cross-references to John's works.

10. For example, he says of those who let their imaginations run wild in prayer and confuse their own imaginings with genuine religious experience: "Some of these people are unbelievably deceived by the devil who will even send them a sort of dew which they suppose to be the heavenly food of angels. It seems to come softly and delicately out of the skies, marvelously finding its way into their mouths. Thus they are in the habit of gaping open-mouthed as if they were trying to catch flies. Make no mistake. All this is an illusion despite its pious overtones, for at the same time their hearts are quite empty of genuine fervor. On the contrary, these weird fantasies have filled them with such vanity that the devil can easily go on to feign odd noises, strange illuminations and delicious odors. It is

a pitiful deceit" (chapter 57; Johnston, p. 122). Clearly the author of the Cloud was somewhat lacking in his ability to "tolerate fools gladly"! And yet I have often laughed aloud while reading the Cloud, something that has never happened with John!

11. Chapter 3; page 48. The page references are to the Johnston Image edition (see footnote 8). Italics added.

12. Chapter 31, pp. 87–88.

13. Chapter 8, pp. 59–60.

14. Chapter 59, p. 126.

15. Chapter 43 p. 102.

16. Chapter 26, p. 83. Balance this description of our struggle to banish distracting thoughts with Teresa's advice simply to ignore distractions once our prayer becomes more passive (see chapter 1 above, pp. 49ff.), unless the distractions become so clamorous that we cannot ignore them. At this stage of prayer, what the author of the Cloud calls "distractions" (pious and zealous reflections about God, ourselves, our world) would not have been distractions at all earlier in our prayer life. Even now, Teresa's advice to simply ignore these pious reflections is probably best; and even that ignoring can be quite a struggle, since our minds resist the vacuum, the cloud of forgetting, which will result if we succeed in ignoring all reflection.

17. Chapter 69, p. 137.

18. Chapter 28, p. 85. See also chapter 69, ad fin., p. 138.

19. Chapter 69, p. 137.

20. Chapter 46, pp. 106–107.

CHAPTER 6

• • •

1. It is surprising, in fact, how little even John and Teresa have to say about the goal of unitive love or the mystical marriage, where the soul and God become truly one and heaven begins, insofar as is possible in this life. For example, the *Living Flame*, which marks the culmination of John's description of the mystical life, has numerous and lengthy digressions concerning the earlier stages of purification. (See Kavanaugh and Rodriguez, p. 574, for several examples.) Even when he does speak of this mystical marriage, John says that God "is usually there, in this embrace with his bride (the soul). . . . Were he always awake within it, communicating knowledge and love, it would already be in glory (in heaven)" (*Living Flame*, Stanza IV, #15; Kavanaugh and Rodriguez, p. 649). It is certain that this total union of love is the ultimate goal of every interior life, indeed of every Christian life. But it is rarely experienced fully in this life, even by the greatest of the saints. What is experienced, if I read John correctly, is a strong but obscure awareness of "God asleep within my boat." Those rare occasions when he awakens are a foretaste of heaven and nearly destroy, in their intensity, the "boat" of our earthly existence.

2. *Dark Night of the Soul*, Book I, chapter X, #4 (Kavanaugh and Rodriguez, p. 317).

3. St. Thérèse of Lisieux, the Little Flower (Santa Teresita in lands with a Spanish heritage), is often confused with St. Teresa of Avila, who founded the Carmelite reform in the sixteenth century with the help of St. John of the Cross. The Little Flower, Thérèse or Teresita, was also a Carmelite and thus a spiritual daughter of Teresa of Avila. (In the charming argot of Carmelites the world over, the Little Flower would refer to Teresa as "our holy mother" and John as "our holy father"; thus, my close association with the Carmelites of Naga—and with John and Teresa—has led them to refer to their founders as my "holy stepmother" and "holy stepfather"! Teresa, who had a great love for the Jesuits, would have been delighted by the adoption.) The confusion between Teresa and Thérèse has been compounded by the fact that both have left us famous autobiographies.

4. Boase explains this paradox of knowing and not knowing, seeing and not seeing, by saying that we have a strong experiential certainty that God is and loves us even though we are totally in the dark as to who or what God is for us (*Prayer of Faith*, pp. 86ff. in the 1950 edition; pp. 76ff. in the 1985 edition).

5. *Dark Night of the Soul*, Book II, chapter VII, #6 (Kavanaugh and Rodriguez, p. 343). John is talking here about the second dark night, that of the spirit. But the soul feels much the same way in the first night of the senses. John begins the very sentence I have quoted above: "Although (the soul) had thought during its first trial that there were no more afflictions which it could suffer, and yet after the trial was over, it enjoyed great blessings, this experience is not sufficient to take

away its belief, during this second trial, that all is now over for it. . . ." See chapter 5, footnote 7 on the distinction and purpose of these two dark nights, and the epilogue on this alternation of light and darkness as the pattern of a mature and deep spirituality.

6. *Dark Night of the Soul*, Book I, chapter XII (Kavanaugh and Rodriguez, pp. 320ff).

7. The reference is to Hannah Hurnard's *Hind's Feet on High Places* and *Mountains and Spices* which we discussed toward the end of chapter 2.

8. John of the Cross discusses this mysterious fact, that we only see our growth when the Lord withdraws his purifying hand. See, for example, the *Dark Night of the Soul*, Book II, chapter VII, #4–6 (Kavanaugh and Rodriguez, pp. 342–343).

9. *Prayer of Faith*, pp. 90ff. in the 1950 edition; pp. 82ff. of the 1985 edition.

10. This is precisely the dilemma we posed for the beginner in prayer in chapters 2 ("The Irrelevance of Prayer") and 3 ("The Relevance of Prayer") of *Opening to God*. The dilemma of the mature prayer is very much the same, but the discernment involved becomes far more subtle. As St. Ignatius says, the devil always enters as an angel of light, tempting us, at every stage of our growth, in ways that then appear good and holy.

11. *Spiritual Exercises*, #21.

EPILOGUE

• • •

1. In *Come Down Zacchaeus*, my book on lay spirituality in the light of Vatican II (Ave Maria Press, 1988), I point out that this latter group of lay disciples is much more numerous in the gospels.

2. Matthew says it was the disciples who criticized them (26:8–9); Mark softens it to "some" (14:4); and John, writing last and perhaps wishing to set the record straight, tells us (12:4) that Judas Iscariot, "the one about to betray him," was the protester.

3. Boase, *The Prayer of Faith*, pp. 106–107 in the 1950 edition; pp. 98–99 in the 1985 edition.

4. This insight was later explored at length in my *Darkness in the Marketplace* (Ave Maria Press, 1981).

5. The phrase "contemplative in action" is often used to describe the apostolic spirituality of St. Ignatius Loyola. For an excellent, brief description of his ideal, see George A. Lane, S.J., *Christian Spirituality*, pp. 62–68 ("Ignatian Prayer: Finding God in All Things"), Argus Communications, 1968.

Thomas H. Green, S.J., is the author of nine books on the spiritual life, including the popular prayer guides *Opening to God* and *Drinking from a Dry Well* (both from Ave Maria Press). An internationally recognized writer, teacher, and mentor, he has served for thirty-seven years at San Jose Seminary in Manila where he is Spiritual Director and Professor of Philosophy and Pastoral Theology. Fr. Green is celebrating fifty-seven years as a member of the Society of Jesus, and fifty years as a missionary in the Philippines. Fr. Green lives in the Philippines.

More Ignatian Favorites

Opening to God
A Guide to Prayer
Thomas H. Green S.J.

For over thirty-four years, *Opening to God* has de-mystified prayer, explaining what prayer is all about and offering techniques that ready the soul to encounter God.
ISBN: 9781594710711 / 128 pages / $10.95

Finding God in Each Moment
The Practice of Discernment in Everyday Life
Carol Ann Smith, S.H.C.J., and Eugene Merz, S.J.

Selections from scripture, writings of St. Ignatius, and documents of Vatican II will lead you to discover how each relationship holds the opportunity to be taught by God.
ISBN: 9781594711008 / 224 pages / $16.95

IGNATIAN IMPULSE SERIES

The Art of Discernment
Making Good Decisions in Your World of Choices
Stefan Kiechle, S.J.

The Art of Discernment is an explanation of the discernment process first developed by St. Ignatius of Loyola: outlining the pros and the cons, considering the decision, listening to our hearts, and doing what is best.
ISBN: 9781594710353 / 128 pages / $9.95

Available from your bookstore or from
ave maria press / Notre Dame, IN 46556
www.avemariapress.com / Ph: 800-282-1865
A Ministry of the Indiana Province of Holy Cross

Keycode: FØAØ8Ø7ØØØØ